NEW POETRY
FROM THE
MIDWEST
2017

NEW POETRY
FROM THE
MIDWEST
2017

OKLA ELLIOTT & HANNAH STEPHENSON
Series Editors

KATHY FAGAN
Final Judge of the 2017 Heartland Poetry Prizes

newamericanpress
Milwaukee, Wis.

n e w a m e r i c a n p r e s s

www.NewAmericanPress.com

Printed in the United States of America

Book design by David Bowen

Cover image (detail) *Untitled* from the series *Hide the Sun*
© 2017 Paula McCartney
www.paulamccartney.com

ISBN 978-1-941561-07-2

For ordering information, please contact:
Ingram Book Group
One Ingram Blvd.
La Vergne, TN 37086
(800) 937-8000
orders@ingrambook.com

For Okla Elliott
(1977-2017)

FOUNDER • EDITOR
WRITER • POET • TEACHER
FRIEND • MENTOR • BROTHER

2017 HEARTLAND POETRY PRIZE WINNERS

"For Peshawar"
by Fatimah Asghar

"The Past Is Alloy, Gigantic"
by Jan Bottiglieri

"David Von Erich Explains the Rules"
by W. Todd Kaneko

Judged by
Kathy Fagan

CONTENTS

HEARTLAND
A Midwestern Poetics Manifesto

Here in the Midwest, we are kind.

Here in the Midwest, we grow things.

Here in the Midwest, we live surrounded by trees and cities, schools and highways, commotion and quiet.

Are these conceptions of the Midwest true? In this year's edition of New Poetry from the Midwest, we do find evidence of the above notions about what it means to be Midwestern, but crucially, we find so much more.

Here in the Midwest, as in the rest of the country, we witness and interrogate suffering and cruelty.

Here in the Midwest, we desire, we yearn.

Here in the Midwest, we question how places and landscape and people shape us, and vice versa.

Everywhere in this anthology, we find generous and imaginative empathy. While this might not be particular to Midwestern poetry, the poems in this volume express empathy with a particular Midwestern earnestness and candor. As Matt Hart puts it, "My dumb green/ heart is wide open." Steve Tomasko confesses, "It hasn't stopped,/ this punch-to-the-gut// feeling, this I-really-am/mortal// feeling…" Fatimah Asghar declares, "Violence/ not an over there but a memory asleep// in our blood, waiting to rise."

Here in the Midwest, we are open, permeable, have allergies.

Here in the Midwest, our traditions are old, our yards, fenced.

Here in the Midwest, we watch.

*

These poems are worried. Appropriately. The news is always on. Is the world ending? Amit Majmudar writes us an "Apocalypse Shopping List." "How strange it feels when one's neighbors/ start disappearing," Jeremy Glazier shares. There are orphans. We fall ill, heal, and fall ill again. We break. Sandra Lindow acknowledges how difficult it is to reconcile language and loss, noting, "Folklorists write/ that the Woman's Journey/ may start with a maiming,/ far easier said on the page/ than felt in the heart's center."

Here in the Midwest, we acquire neighbors, students and teachers, friends, lovers, partners, children.

Here in the Midwest, as in all the world, those we come to love, leave. Always too soon.

Here in the Midwest, we remember.

This past spring, we lost our friend and co-editor, Okla Elliott. Before he passed away, he and I worked carefully to collect these words, to showcase the beauty that we know Midwestern authors contribute to our world. Okla was a friend to a staggering number of writers and readers. He believed in radical empathy; he believed in the truth and power of language(s); he believed in the necessity of art for survival in the face of tragedy and trauma.

I know that you believe this, too. These poems want you to be nourished and comforted, even (especially) in dark days. Gingerbread crumbs, egg yolk, baba ghanoush, crunchy lunch apple, golden honey, coffee, cocoa. Grit, sweat, soil, blood.

Read further, friend. We do not say goodbye here. We say, welcome. Bring your green heart and your wounds, your fears, your bright memories. Drink deeply, feel, and know: you and we are not alone.

—Hannah Stephenson

Susan Aizenberg

* * *

JULY AT ROSE BLUMKIN

—*Memory Unit, Home for the Aged*

Even this early in the morning,
heat breathes heavily against the panes
and the light's a white flame that warps
the glass of this picture window
overlooking the "wander garden"

and its border of young maples and beyond them—
I swear—gravestones rising

from the mist in the cemetery
just across the road. We've arrived
to find your father dozing here,
in the television room, deaf
to the chattering loop of *Lucy* reruns

flickering the big screen and the rhythmic
nonstop barking of the woman

slumped in the wheelchair
closest to it. At ninety-two, his skin's
almost translucent and his arms
are mottled with bruises the bitter
purple of ruined eggplants, and nearly

that large, a sorry map of needle sticks
and places where he's rested too long

against his walker. When he wakes
he knows us, but not our names,
what year it is, or how to call up sense
and syntax from the ruptured channels
harrowing his brain. Not all

he says is gibberish: *This is the shits,*
he tells us. *We're not doing this again.*

A man named Buddy, still dapper
in pressed jeans and a turtleneck, agrees.
Some daughter must do his laundry.
Mostly the men and women here
are incontinent, and like your father,

mostly they refuse to eat.
The young nurses are kind,

some of them lovely, as they crush pills
into applesauce for spoon-feeding,
offer juice boxes, and speak softly
to their charges, who doze
and nod, tremulous as dandelion puffs,

on the stalks of their necks.
It's hard to leave, and you give your father

*

your hand, tell him how many days
it will be until you return.
He repeats the number, *three*,
and seems to understand, and though all
his life he was a man uneasy

with affection, now bends
to kiss your fingers, courtly and sad.

FIRST PUBLISHED IN *QUIET CITY*

Marilyn Annucci

* * *

THE SMALLEST BONES

1. Anvil

Under glass in the museum
you are small and white, a baby

tooth no fairy collects, and far
from the ear out of which you were

extracted. Incus, your Latin
name—the hard k hones

you, keeps your roots pointed
down, sharp as a fingernail

in a dark glove, in a dark
canal, vibrating.

2. Stirrup

The horses have gone off
without you, unsaddled, unbridled,

hooves like hollow mugs of wood.
If one could shrink and stand

beneath your tiny roman arch,
one might hear them, how they

echo across the cobbles, past
the high walls, as if the palace

were destination. The drum
distant and somewhere else.

And you, with your history,
your languages unrecoverable.

3. Hammer

You make audible the whisper,
the hush, whatever false phrases

linger behind fingers that eclipse
the mouth. What hesitates

to enter the coiled corridors
of the cochlea, arrives.

With your furious fang you stare
down romantics who metamorphose

knives into flutes, boulders into songs.
What isn't heard clearly the first time

*

you repeat, you repeat, you repeat
until what has come through one ear

is nailed, cannot come out the other.

FIRST PUBLISHED IN *ANTIPHON*

Fatimah Asghar

* * *

FOR PESHAWAR

December 16th, 2014

Before attacking schools in Pakistan,
the Taliban sends kafan, *a marking*
of Muslim burials, as a way of psychological terror.

The white linen arrives to a school
to warn of the approaching funeral.

A gift to begin wrapping the bodies.
They send flowers before guns now

all the thorns plucked from the stems.
An order to weave the dirge

before the mortar sings. The moment
our babies are born, are we meant

to lower them into the ground?
Every year I manage to live on this earth

I collect more questions than I do answers.
In my dreams, the children are still alive

at school. In my dreams they still play
unaware of what is coming.

———

I wish them only a mundane life.
Arguments with parents. Groundings.

Chasing a budding love around the playground.
Iced mango slices in the hot summer.

Lassi dripping from their lips.
Fear of being unmarried. Hatred of the family

next door. Kheer at graduation. Fingers licked
with mehndi. Blisters on the back of a heel.

Pulling hair off a friend's arm.
Loneliness in a bookstore. Fingerprints

on spine. Walking home with the sun
at their backs. Searching the street

for a missing glove. Nothing glorious.
I promise. Just, alive.

Please.

--/--

I lose track of whom I am begging.
Each please

a vast cave I fear when its depths answer.

I scream

& hear only the sound of my own haunting.
I will believe

in any god that offers me a new beginning.
I will believe

in any god: man, metal or magic.

———

My friend's voice lands, a bird shriveled with sorrow.
She is visiting the houses that once had children.

We are too busy trying to separate the good terrorists
from the bad.

The line hums. The silence a simmer across mountains.
Again, I hear the bird ruffle its wings. A worm twists
in my throat.

How do you kill someone who isn't afraid of dying?

The line hums.

   --/--

I didn't know I needed to worry
about them until they were gone.

--/--

My uncle gifts me his youngest memory:
              a parking lot full of bodies

screams & a forest waiting to protect.
              In all our family histories, one wrong

turn & then, death. Violence
              not an over there but a memory asleep

in our blood, waiting to rise.
              We know this from our nests—

the bad men wanting to end us.
              Every year, we call them something new.

British. Americans. Indians. Hindus. Terrorists.
              The steady dirge of our hearts pounding

vicious, as we prepare the white
              linen, as we ready to wrap our bodies.

FIRST PUBLISHED IN *THE MARGINS*

Fatimah Asghar

* * *

SUPER ORPHAN

Today, I donned my cape like a birth
certificate & jumped, arms wide into the sky.

-

Woke up, parents still
dead. Outside, the leaves yawn,

re-christen themselves as spring.

-

I know—once there was a man.
Or maybe a woman.

Let's try again: once, there was a family.
What came first?

-

What to do then, when the only history
you have is collage?

-

Lets try again. Once there was a village
on a pale day, unaware of the greatness

at its gate.

-

Today, I woke:
Batman, a king over Gotham.

The city sinning at my feet
begging to be saved.

-

The same dream again:
police running after my faceless
family with guns

my uncle leaps into a tulip
filled field, arms turning to wings
as bullets greet him.

-

Today, I woke, slop-lipped
and drunk, cards in my hand,

*

Joker in my chest. Today I woke
angry at the world for its hurt

wanting to make more like me.

-

Are all refugees superheroes?

Do all survivors carry villain inside them?

-

Today, I donned my cape like a birth
certificate & jumped, arms wide into the sky.

-

How else to say I am here?

FIRST PUBLISHED IN *THE MARGINS*

Sayuri Ayers

* * *

YEARS AFTER

> ...*yes my mountain flower...*
> —Molly (*Ulysses*)

Each night our house
empties itself of trouble
as all the small things scuttle out,
beetles from the shag rug
silverfish from bookshelves.
As you sleep I patch wormholes
with plaster, caulk crevices
in pearly loops. Our bedroom walls
tremble with mastication:
cockroaches gnawing on fingernail
clippings, termites on pine studs.
As our house crumbles
I whisper in your ear *yes*—
as if it all could be
reborn like a grafted blood
orange sprig, rewoven
hymen. As you drift half-
drunk, I rummage through
junk drawers, pairing
knives and forks. I count
off my lovers on each tine.
My heart leans inside of

me, laden with unpicked fruit.
The earwig in the cupboard
shudders, squeezing out
the first of her golden brood.

FIRST PUBLISHED IN *WACCAMAW*

Julie Babcock

* * *

RULES FOR REARRANGEMENT

a.   Introduce your new self and explain your need. For instance: I need to build security. For instance: I need to box memories. I need to let my objects know it's not them.

b.   Rearrangement involves more than just one variable. The guitar from the chair and at different times of day when the sun opens and closes its boxes across the planks.

c.   Empty space you uncover will be awkward and shy. Swab it clean and assure: I see you. You are here and welcome. I am sorry you had to hide. I am sorry you missed the sun, the wind, and music.

d.   Former free space you cover will be angry. It will warp the planks until you trip. It will tilt and spill your drinks. Drop frames until they shatter. There is nothing you can do to soothe it. Look past the mutinies and never yield. You rearrange to survive. That hurricane and then you. The new Captain and Commander of Sacrifice.

FIRST PUBLISHED IN *WESTERN HUMANITIES REVIEW*

Julie Babcock

* * *

SHE SHALL SOON FIND A WAY

Gingerbread after an exile. After the funeral pyre has smoked down and
the last bread crumbs
    stolen. How sweet now to have found this forest

house, ground cinnamon and ginger, spiced bark and root, a revival. Of
course she eats it.
Life belongs to whoever can find it, to whomever

keeps walking and trying. Children know this. That eating one door leads
to another. That
    when captured. . .

She grabs a handful of gingerbread cake, lines her pockets with crispy
cookies, licks icing
    along a window. She is what she does. She is

a molasses-dark shape in the trees.

FIRST PUBLISHED IN *WEAVE*

Melissa Barrett

WFM: ALLERGIC TO PINE SOL, AM I THE ONLY ONE

—lines from Craigslist personal ads

Hi. I react really badly to Pine-Sol. My eyelids swell up and my eyes
turn bright red. I am a REAL woman. It is January 1, 2014.
Educated men move to the top of the list.
We were both getting gas Wednesday evening. Fish counter, Giant Eagle:
My husband knows how attractive I find you.
You caught me singing loudly. Your name means "wind."
This Christmas season marks my eighth year of being single.
Please have a car (truck preferably) and a job.
I collect candles and have two grown children who are on their own now
thank God. I already bought your birthday present—
It's a tie. With swordfish on it. There are certain things
my nose can't handle and smoking is one of them.
I signed up to volunteer at a local park for a Merry not Scary
trick or treat trail—it would be nice to have a companion.
Must be willing to be seen in public with a size 16 woman.
I'm a little bigger, but not sloppy-fat. Six one four five eight
two three one nine. I can swing a hammer and am a pro
at putting on make-up. Sexiness to me is you
plus a photographic memory. Do you have questions
you've always wanted to ask a woman? You left your receipt
and that's how I figured out your name. I was behind you
at the Lane Avenue Starbucks drive thru and you paid
for my grande nonfat, no whip Mocha Frapp.

Your silver hair was gorgeous. Wow. The first time
we made love our souls connected and intertwined
and seemed to remember they were destined for one another.
Let's go to the shooting range. I have no business expertise,
but I'd love a guy who is good with rope.

FIRST PUBLISHED IN *THE JOURNAL*

Michael Bazzett

* * *

THE CITY

Once we were ten miles outside the city, it
vanished completely. We suspected this
happened from the top down, with television
antennae fading into ether and asphalt
shingles glimmering, like fish scales,
then flecking into nothingness.
                    For a mere
moment buildings were reduced to ribcage,
people illuminated within the lattice of beams,
bent over ironing boards and countertops,
chopping cucumbers into slender green coins
until they and their knives and even the blade-
scarred board had vanished into empty air.

But there were also those who asserted
buildings softened into something like
sodden cardboard and settled slowly into
themselves. One contingent even claimed
nothing happened at all: the city simply
shifted like a sleeping animal, dreaming
of our return.
        We decided to confirm
our top-down theory by hiding a camera
in the woven branches of a linden tree
then climbing into our van and driving
until the city sank into the dusky horizon.

*

There, someone said, pointing, it's done it again.

And it was true, the impassive brick and steel
were gone. We cranked a U-turn and rumbled
home over the asphalt we'd just traveled
in hopes of catching our city in the breathless
unclothed moment before she had once again
reassembled herself, down to bits of rusted
hardware on the roadside and the actors
hired to loiter outside of bars.
    But this time,
as we coasted slowly into our neighborhood,
past the imposters and hastily reconstructed
but nonetheless convincing details, we smiled
quietly at one another.

    The van creaked to a stop under the tree
and we leaned the ladder into its thick crown

when suddenly something lifted
scraping into flight, croaking
like a rusted door—

as if the tree had cracked
open and coughed its dark and broken
heart into the sky—

FIRST PUBLISHED IN *THE JOURNAL*

Michael Bazzett

* * *

TONGUES

Most people can already speak
hurricane, given that it's mostly howling

rage and shares numerous
cognates with the mother tongue.

But sunlight
is a quiet dialect

where every word sounds
almost the same to the untuned

eye. It is native
only to the green leaves
that devour it whole.

FIRST PUBLISHED IN *NINTH LETTER*

Jeffrey Bean

* * *

KID, THIS IS OCTOBER,

you can make the maples blaze
just by stopping to look,
you can set your clock to the barks
of geese. Somewhere the grandfathers
who own this town lean down to iron
crisp blue shirts, their faces bathing
in steam, and blackbirds
clamor in packs,
make plans behind corn.
You know this,
you were born whistling
at crackling stars, you snap
your fingers and big turtles
slide out of rivers to answer.
You can swim one more time
in the puddle of sun
in your water glass, taste icicles
already in the white crunch
of your lunch apple. Go
to sleep. I'll put on my silver suit
and chase the sky into the moon.

FIRST PUBLISHED IN *MISSOURI REVIEW*

Jeffrey Bean

* * *

KID, THIS IS IOWA,

everything we are is here—
my dead grandmother as a girl
hunting fireflies in tiger lilies,
me throwing walnuts at gas cans
by the barn, stomping mud puddles,
my sticky hands lifting an apple
to my mouth. Here are dogwoods
and hills of corn that lead to more hills
of corn and more corn until the moon
comes up hot and my father
rattles the ice in his gin and tonic,
polishes his guitar. The horses
that dragged the lumber to build
my grandparents' house still stomp
in the back pasture, swirl their tails
at fat, biting flies, and the sizzle of bacon
keeps waking me from my childhood
dreams: cattails snapping
their fingers, a badger's green stare
caught in headlights, my grandfather's
riding mower humming on the lawn,
confetti of clipped grass stuck
to his neck. The clouds here are so long
they stretch from the hidden parts of your blood
across the Atlantic to some lost place where

every ocean is healthy again, plump with whales,
and your forbears stand on cobblestones
around a barrel fire, licking
salted whitefish off their thumbs.
And here you are this morning, climbing
the wood fence I will always carry splinters from,
lifting your body into the smoke of
our leaf fire, great plumes of it reminding us
we were born to keep moving here, keep
leaving here, keep killing these fields and hills,
twisting them into smoke, then bringing them back.

FIRST PUBLISHED IN *MISSOURI REVIEW*

Roy Bentley

* * *

SIX-DEGREE FREEDOM

> *Big black road, big black river,*
> *big black Heaven in the sky above...*
> —Patti Scialfa, "Big Black Heaven"

It's 1965. We're about a mile up, maybe more.
The pilot is I.T. since his name is Ivan Taylor.
I.T.'s decided I'm the son that he'll never have.
All summer, he's been taking me up; letting me,
just this week, fly. Steer the thing straight and
level through a bright world above the world.
Below, a checkerboard of corn- and beanfields:
a white-striped snake of two-lane I recognize
as the shortcut past the Pure Oil refinery.
I.T.'s got on those aviator Ray-Bans. He's
Johnny Unitas, in profile—cropped hair,
one of those grief-chiseled, movie-star faces
that you expect nothing, and everything, of.
He's telling me about six-degree freedom,
holding forth about roll, pitch, yaw—whatever
those are—and up and side. Which takes me
somewhere I don't want to be in the Cessna.
He says, "Pay attention. This is backward,"
and slows our forward momentum mid-air.

———————

*

I.T.'s warming up, throwing first base to third,
the shortstop catching whatever is left over.
Coach Woody Hayes is at Ohio State, and so
every pick-up game is war. Life and death.
You know these guys—sixteen-seeming at thirty.
At forty. The shortstop hurries a practice tag,
reminding I.T. that he's reminding himself
to press. I know this guy, he thinks, staring
into the ball diamond of I.T.'s Ray-Bans.
Then—wham!—I.T.'s into the near-infield
grass, one-kneeing what should have been easy.
He's gone down for. In the Hoback Park bleachers
I.T.'s wife is beside me. Pat doesn't like baseball,
hard seats. A car radio plays a Buck Owens song.
The song is about having a tiger by the tail.

————————

I.T.'s from No Lie, Kentucky. South of,
and between, Hell for Certain and Jenkins.
A hillbilly, technically, because any hillbilly
with college is like a man without a country.
He's been called briarhopper once or twice.
In the air, we're off course. Not by much
but enough that I.T. touches the bent brim
of his ballcap. Stares at the line of sunset-
as-horizonline. He's decided something
isn't where it was before, and we turn,
the dials of the control panel beginning
to blaze, greening in advancing dark.

————————

From my side of the plane, I see a worked-
to-curving brim of ballcap, some lettering—
everything there is to know about Ivan Taylor
landing a Cessna. If Sundin's Flight School
had lighted runways I'd know this happened
all the time, right-stuff pilots going farther out
than one should on allotted fuel. I'd reconstruct
an airstrip so lit up by a gas station's signage
that it should be no sweat. Piece of cake.
If I could trace the line of athleticism
from an infield pop fly I.T. bare-handed
for the final inning's side-retiring out,
to this windscreen, I'd keep I.T.'s American cool
like it was my birthright or a lucky silver dollar.
I'd have the right-side profile of a man—
all men who exhaust themselves and their allotment
of luck in the service of—what?—you tell me.
The most familiar place in the world is what
we have to get back to, acres of wheat and alfalfa
knotting the last of the light and Heath, Ohio.

———————

I'm not thinking of the Wright Brothers
when Pat hands I.T. his 30th birthday present.
And I'm tired of the happy pictures of families
sitting down to peaceful meals in the nineteen sixties.
I'm weary of hearing how awfully good it was then.
Maybe any part of the truth travels better, farther,
than the whole truth. It's just that Ivan Taylor

pitching his unopened gift onto a sofa cushion
isn't anything I've seen before. This is the year
it will come crashing down for both of them,
the year I kill Pat's oldest and favorite parakeet,
lobbing the bird-as-baseball to Garry Bowling,
a neighbor kid. Don't ask me why I did that.
Ask I.T. about winging that ribboned shirt box.

———————

Here we are: downwind of—scared, you bet—
and directly over the restaurant where Pat works.
I can see the high schoolers cruising, rolling
through the restaurant parking lot, circling,
while sweating herds of Holstein cattle
fill a flat quilt of fields before the airport.
I.T. isn't happy about any of this—his life
going totally bust, having to put both hands
on the lopped-off figure-eight of the wheel,
bracing to take whatever comes. To his right,
I await the usual touching-down cry of tires.
He turns from what he's doing to tell me
something I can't hear over the high whine
of the Cessna's throttling up. He looks back,
hydraulic sighings and gear-grindings underfoot
a kind of signal (must be) because he brakes.
And hard enough to leave a ribbon of black
to testify to the fact we're down, and safe.
We taxi to the hanger and I.T. flips the engine
kill switch. We sit in a silence almost Biblical.
He points in the direction of an almond of flame

from the burning off of waste gases at the refinery.
The light's no big deal. What's local never is.
And then he says, That's what I had to steer by
as if letting a boy in on more than he should.

FIRST PUBLISHED IN *CHAGRIN RIVER REVIEW*

Monica Berlin

* * *

UNTITLED

What happens is this: the body calls—though we don't

call it that, say Small or Button, say O, say hey coming to.
What happens is the body rings another body, think orbit,

& no matter later than we thought. What happens
in the difference of time—& nothing to undo that

distance, those two thousand thirty miles, those twenty-
eight highway hours, if no traffic & no stopping, &

seven state lines & a landscape gone from maple & birch
to mountain & drop-off to desert to oceanside & palm

-treed & bayshore—is one side of a warmed bed, is
darkening night, is quiet deepening to still.

& what's to say but just nodded off, what's to say but
your voice the pillow—. What's to say but here, but you.

Think always, the planets we can't see but trust there.
Think physics, pull & sound & force & light &

everything we move by without understanding. Think
no day a day until—. What happened was we tried

*

calling it nothing, tried lapse of judgment & never mind
& passing time & impossible, but then sudden years.

So we named this river, called it floatation device, said raft
& buoy & anchor, said sandbag, said high water mark. Said

a rope. Tried windbreak & treeline & prairie. Called it book
of every day & folded a page. Called it early morning

where sometimes through gauzy curtains we watch sky
brighten. Called it turned-down bed. Tried afternoon, tried

and, tried hunger or tired, said tomorrow, said ours. How to
name this every door left opened & waiting, this every hour

a window staring out, when what we mean is sharp cornering
of elbow, bend of knee, is the wrist's ulna, the wrist's

radius, fingers tracing scapula, my mouth against
your clavicle, when what we mean is held & hold & hand

& handling & keep talking & stay awhile & enough sometimes
to hear your breath slow on the other end of any line.

FIRST PUBLISHED IN *CINCINNATI REVIEW*

Tom Boswell

* * *

AFTER READING THE FIRST POEM
IN THE LITERARY JOURNAL,
I STOP TO CONTEMPLATE LIFE AND DEATH

It was a good strong poem. About how someone
had died and all his friends had gathered at the pub

to ponder his passing and that time-worn mystery
of where we all go when we are gone. The world

is turning towards spring as I flip to the back

of the journal to peruse the listing of publications,
awards and brief bio. But the poet is past tense.

He died of cancer in November, never saw in print
this good strong poem about him and friends drinking

to the memory of their deceased companion.

Next week I start a new job, my first 9-to-5 in decades.
For years now, the days have been rushing by like …

well, the newly-dead poet said it best: like bats at dusk.
The way they whoosh across the darkening sky,

webbed wing-hands fluttering too fast to see.

Each day I make a list of things to do and at day's end,
to my disgust, I've checked off just a few. Now here,

mocking me in this pile of unread magazines,
the latest issue of AARP, (did I subscribe?) with the

cover story: Find a New Job: Make Yourself Relevant.

I'd like to think I had been, but now I'm wondering
if the dead poet, had he known he wouldn't live

to see this last poem published, might have chosen
a different piece to go out with, perhaps one about ice

cracking on a creek in spring, chickadees chirping

in the morning, the first blush of green on a lilac shrub
or a crocus pushing its nose through snow, rather than this

good strong poem about him and his buddies drinking
to a friend's demise, wondering where we go when we leave

here, what's on the other side of life, and those bats at dusk.

FIRST PUBLISHED IN *GLASS MOUNTAIN*

Jan Bottiglieri

* * *

THE PAST IS ALLOY, GIGANTIC

There was a motorcycle—cobalt blue
plastic, about 16 inches high, white handlebars.
My son rode it, a mad abandon, clacking
in our basement, down the sidewalk, no engine
but the legs he used to have, attached
to the body he used to have, small and milk-stuffed.
Where are you going? I'd ask, folding laundry.
I'm going to see my old mommy. This was the '90s:
what did we have then? Chlorofluorocarbons,
Apple IIs. It was hip-hop's Golden Age.
He called it "mugger-cycle." His riding was a sea.
This was a long time ago, to him and me.

The past is alloy, gigantic. Nothing goes away.
Everything is somewhere, my old mother
used to say. Your windbreaker did not grow legs
and walk off by itself. I went back to the park:
there it was, pockets stuffed with seedpods
I'd gathered, a finite universe. Bee-velvet,
the twitching rabbit I'd stalked: that was that day.
I already carried the cells that would be my son.

*

Petroleum waited beneath that Earth to become
the plastic; before that, as algae—leafless, Paleozoic—
it drank sun, that simple ardor. It could never
not be. Like boy, body, jacket, riding, sea.

FIRST PUBLISHED IN *ALLOY*

Traci Brimhall

* * *

BEDTIME STORY WITH GOODNIGHT MOON AND CNN

Here, the now turns the cardboard pages to telephones
and red balloons. Goodnight moon. Goodnight room.

There, in the then, a scarecrow stuffed with a missing
woman's hair. There in the web, a wolf spider

with a September hunger and blind in half her eyes.
Back, back in your newest hour, a woman vanished

and no one looked for her. Dark, dark my stalk and tassel.
Darker still my shadow's voice reciting newborn gospels,

ardent as the sing and saw of wind. Goodnight nobody.
Goodnight mush. Rock, rock in a stippled field. Rock and hush

as the rest of the woman is found abandoned in Indiana.
As others are discovered in positions of sleep or rapture

in buildings tagged for demolition. Who knows how many
we could find, the officer says as teams sweep the empty blocks.

He targeted women no one would miss. Before confessions,
my relief. I would miss your nose, your ears, your sour

*

breath, therefore you are safe. Therefore, emergency
numbers secure on the fridge, the reassurance of curtains.

Goodnight air. Goodnight noises everywhere. Soft, soft
the windfall apples. Softer still the curled fists gripping

the yes of the world, accepting the television's cadence
of tragedy and the sleepless months revised into happiness,

the yes of flies corseting a body, the yes of trees thriving
in the cemetery. Yes, the moon. Its bright, unending yes.

FIRST PUBLISHED IN *NARRATIVE*

Joshua Butts

* * *

RIVERFRONT NO. 1

after George Bellows (1915)

Squashed people. Spot the dandy. I might huddle.
I might bend with crack. I might hang. I might stand
arms akimbo in row boat. I might set up, necklace
my only ornament. I might dry. I might captain
a ship. I might climb the pier my full buttocks showing.
I might shadow and talk. A dot for an eye speaking
to a dot for an eye. I might lie down, my back
in full sun but for when clouds press by. I might
bring my child, my sister. I might lose this denim
and walk home in full skin. I might tuck my knees.
I might curse the heat and dip into the cold, careful
for the pier. I might glower in blue shorts. I might scratch
my knee. I might dive. I might line up to dive. I might
freeze here in the cold sea. I might shuffle. I might wear
green pants. I might be a sail. I might be a freighter.
I am knuckles for arms. I might take a last look slip in.
I might fall asleep with gray straps crossing my shoulders.
There could be a nickel in my pocket. There could be a whole
cord for fire. (I stack it far from the shore to keep dry.)
What if I were somebody else? This boy next to me,
or that boy, or that woman hanging from the pier?
What if I were dejected in trunks? What if I were nude
and wearing a necklace? What if I were smoke feeding

a cloud? Hold yourself against me what would you find?
A cat might step over me. What if I were perspective
and went missing? What if I am passed out naked figure left,
passed out naked figure right? Am I passed out or am I
drowned, a blue hull? I am limbs. I am assemblage.
A blurred breast. I rise and deny I was ever here. I rise and deny
that I was anywhere else. I rise and deny and rise and deny
for I am made of oil. I am not realism. I check my knee.
I wear a blue skirt. I have friends. I'm so tall a haberdasher
called me Tree. I hold my sister's arm. She holds her toddler.
Is there a better place to bathe than the riverfront? I am
orange trunk suit. I am drying off. Hold me close against you.

FIRST PUBLISHED IN *BURNSIDE REVIEW*

Joshua Butts

* * *

OUR ÁNTONIA

Cut open the sky
and let the pill bottle

drop through,
a shake sound

as it falls to the twigs.
The bottle finds a girl,

long hair tucked
around a broad face.

Tell us the heart-kill.
Let the blue air feed

at least tobacco.
Your father will

hang the violin
on the wall and then hang

on the wall.
Give us a bib or

*

a Bible.
Those clothes are flipping

through your brain.
We could crumble thru—

pick up some beer.
We could save you

if you were able to stop
the dryer. Most of all

don't lose desire
in a towheaded family.

We are only the blanket.
You are the golden plain.

FIRST PUBLISHED IN *TAMPA REVIEW*

Kai Carlson-Wee

* * *

MINNESOTA ROADS

Dawn light and I'm driving the back-country dairies
and hayricks on North 64, my brother asleep
on the window beside me. The radio tuned
to an alt-country station they stream
out of Walker-Laporte. Fog over everything.
Wheels and ditch-grass. Broken machinery
rusting away in the yards. Satellites shine
now and then in the lifting dark. Headlights align
with the fences and trail off, haunted
like fishing boats trolling the point.
Everything stalks to the edge of the morning
and waits. Even our car seems to slide
on the cusp of a barely invisible screen.
Hinting at some kind of wilder country the silos
have always kept hidden from view—
squatting an open-air flatcar in Portland,
opening tin cans of stewed prunes and tuna fish,
fireworks blooming the eastern Montana sky.
Thinking of Olaf alone in the mountains now.
Kerri-Ann living on food stamps in Bellingham.
Severson army-bound. Zeidlhack dead.
Barron locked up in a steel-plate cell for the next
six years of his life. Somewhere near Wilmar
the sun hits the trees and my brother
wakes up to the glare. Townes on the radio.

Crows on the power lines passing beside us
in waves. I dreamt of a mutated cowboy,
he tells me. A man without fingers, but still
having hands. I pass him the rest of our Zig-Zags
and shaker. He takes out the rumpled-up atlas
and rolls down the window to let in some air.

FIRST PUBLISHED IN *Narrative*

Sarah Carson

* * *

WHAT WE DO IN VEHICLE CITY

We live in a world now where anything can happen, in a town too big
for just one sister city, street corners so full of possibilities boys spin in
circles; their fathers decided this place was not enough like the flyer; they
had followed a whole trail of discarded things north to a location stripped
bare of its tree trunks, where men threw wrenches out of open windows
until all of the cops were gone. Now we all have dreams that we're at
a party in Billy Durant's driveway when someone starts pulling up the
shrubbery around the carriage house. An AM/FM radio finds its way
out an upstairs window and shorts out the lights in the big, expensive
swimming pool. The police arrive and we begin to run the way we are
always running in dreams. We find a car waiting by the sidewalk, take it
east to where the plains roll up into hillsides, where the car starts groaning
and shaking and quitting and we are angry and we keep saying, "This is
not what we do in America. This is no way to make a getaway. This is the
reason no one knows if the buried are really dead."

FIRST PUBLISHED IN *MINNESOTA REVIEW*

George David Clark

* * *

TRAVELING CIRCUS

It's midnight when I slip into the elephant's stockade,
and with the sky black I find the pachyderms by scent.
Gently, I shush them and unscrew their trunks
so the wind spills out of those generous skulls.
At their sagging thighs I kneel to roll them up
like sleeping bags until they fit in a sleeve for nickels.

In the dressing room's icy windows icy candles shrink.
My handkerchief rainbows as I scrub the face paint off the clowns.
Under their makeup they're still laughing, but not with their mouths
or their eyes. I clean an inch of blue off here,
of pink off there, and soon they're just the eight white pawns
from an heirloom chess set, docile and stoic as thumbs.

The stilts telescope. The big top folds and folds.
My shirt is the lion inside out, his canines for the cufflinks.
When I've vacuum-sealed the acrobats within their leotards,
I use a high wire to tether the tent stakes. And as morning nears,
I trim my moustache in the funhouse mirror before stowing
the glass in my briefcase with the spotlights and everything else.

By the all-but-empty boulevard the contortionist waits
in her long red dress, holding our drowsy taxi. We kiss
and she straightens my tie. Couldn't we stay a little longer, I ask her.
A smile is her reply. Then as she slowly disarticulates,

she whispers our itinerary town by town, tender as a lullaby:
Philly then Pittsburgh, Detroit to St. Paul.

Every time, I fear that something's been forgotten,
likely the sign that begs applause. Did we even remember
to perform last night? My love ignores my worry.
Smaller and smaller she wrinkles and squints. Then we're already gone
and all morning she'll hum like half a ticket stub in my left
breast pocket till my heart vibrates: Chicago, Chicago, Chicago.

FIRST PUBLISHED IN *CINCINNATI REVIEW*

Patricia Clark

* * *

FRONTAL VIEW OF TREES

after Wolf Kahn

I like it when the trunks
                of the birches
        take up earth's
    mantis green,
that's what she would do—
                appropriate the ground,
        by sinking in.

She troubles me, my mother
                who didn't die
        comforted, at home.
    Our bodies, fates
we live but cannot decipher.
                The sun offers
        its warming touch.

Souls of the dead, thin
                presences and pale—
        yet their spirits
    have turned to light—
glow of cumin, cinnamon ruddy
                in the corner
        of the canvas.

*

To misread means to author
                your own text—
     in truth, the trunks
   wear flood marks, mud
floating high in water left
             the smear.
    She fell down.

Smack of the ground's kiss,
            that broke
   her nose. The doctor said,
  dead before she hit the ground.
Linked once, she and I severed now
               and who will be
    at my side when I go?

The birches make a grove
            collecting light—
   she wore a verve
  for living, cloak
of many colors.

FIRST PUBLISHED IN *CIMARRON REVIEW*

Patricia Clark

* * *

THE SLIT

Thought I saw, at the day's start,
        a door open in an oak tree—
a vertical slit, a magical port—
            a figure stood there,
then disappeared—
      I could neither follow
      nor lie about the journey.

See how the light fills chamber and halls
      in the woods here?
The suggestion makes a church,
          narthex, nave, a place
for worship if you trust
      where your eyes
      take you, up and up.

Thought I knew when a leaf stood still
      something mirrored there,
the margin, toothed, irregular,
          and the oblong shape
    with veins spreading out like streams,
      where an estuary fills,
drains, makes a birthing place.

*

Where I did not lie down, a forest floor
        of mayapple, trillium, moss.
Birdcall of bluejay came with a laugh,
                        others unidentified—
    one a phrase curling up
        at the end like sword fern,
then down, phrase two complete. Wood thrush?

Imagined I glimpsed, in light indistinct and fogged
                    with time, a door in a white oak
crack open, close, the way a cell
                changes or allows a thing
    in—an ort of food, speck
        of water for the tree's throat,
bit of DNA ragged, flawed.

Someone ascended, believe if you will,
        a winding stair with no handrail,
found a place within, staying,
                never emerging,
    a woodsy sequestering with bark,
                duff for insulation—
breathing silence, rustling, watching beyond words.

FIRST PUBLISHED IN *KENYON REVIEW*

Heidi Czerwiec

* * *

IV.

from SWEET/CRUDE: A Bakken Boom Cycle

North Dakota is a foreign country. Alien. A flyover state, even from
space. When we show our foreign friend a photo of a satellite flyover,
he's astonished. At nightfall, light clusters on the frozen prairie,
phantom city emerged from among the ghost towns. A blooming
midnight meridian. Stars in a lake of blackness, a constellation of
ignited eyes. The natural gas that emerges alongside the oil costs more
to capture than flare. The foreign companies that drill here burn money,
a billion a year in flames and fines. A Little Kuwait on the Prairie
whose dread watchfires smelter under the dark more brightly than
Minneapolis. More broadly than Chicago. In winter, truckers cluster
for warmth beneath the flares, which fling their flapping rags of fire six
yards into space, toward the stars and satellites and passing planes.
Foreigner, flyover passenger, when you peer out your window, what do
you see? What lies beneath you?

FIRST PUBLISHED IN *ELEVEN ELEVEN*

Krista DeBehnke

* * *

FINGER OF GOD IN BELVIDERE, ILLINOIS, 1967

I.

It doesn't sound like a freight train. If gray was a sound
it would fill our ears and if gray was solid
it would fill our eyes and it might be peace
if we could hold it and keep it safe
and it might be safe
like how soft those clouds looked
from the bus stop, not pins and needles
of cold water and no air left to breathe.

II.

We like April when it's not cruel,
We like Illinois April without coats,
and catching the early country bus
to Immanuel Lutheran Elementary
and we should have prayed for April
a gift given without request,
just a day with a little more body,
a little less warning.

III.

The air was jealous or my eyes were too Irish
because all I saw was green tint
in my hair and on my skin.
Envy spit something into a field

and the air contemplated
and the air waited for the right move
and the air was fury trapped in a tight space
and yet, and yet,
we cannot worship false gods.

IV.
Becky was extra safe
and we must be too
in the seats behind the bus driver;
they'll always save their side first.

In the mist of funnels and gray
the door opened and the driver left
maybe up like a gull
or a skipping stone across the field—
his bald head must have shone
like a crucifix bobbing through corn
and wheat, saving himself
so he couldn't save anyone.

Becky in the first seat had eyes
like half-moons and a mouth
full of almost-smiles
she said goodbye to the driver
but didn't really say anything—
the new protector with all of her
eight years, waiting for the grown-ups
like her mama taught her.

V.

That finger of god stole my purse
from my shoulder and my baseball
glove, straight up into the gray—hair clip,
latchkey, lunch money and broken zipper
gone to decorate his nest of trinkets.
He must have needed it—arm
up-stretched in the no gravity of
a thousand balloons, a barrage
of gravel against shins and toenails
made me kneel to the messenger.
And yet, he really wanted nothing
which was all the fun of it.

VI.

I came to in cold rain,
in the mean smell of blood,
I welcomed no homes.
The last tree bowed to the boy
asleep face-down in the mud
and I cried no noise
for another boy with a pipe
through his thigh, my mouth in howl
like all of his sisters reciting names
of the found in a low hum of recognition—
sister, sister, brother brother,
sister, brother, sister, brother—
little satellites, their only job
is to look for signal.

VII.

We pick and choose
the best treats, the pinkest
tea cups in the china store,
we opt for the cherry within
the chocolate. Saturn waited
on top of the radio tower
devouring the dead boy's pants,
twenty houses, twenty people,
but not another son. The best
are the first to go. I must not
think my sister's name.

VIII.

Station-wagon ambulance, school-door
stretcher, teenage paramedics, driver's
siren of *get out of the way,*
I've got dying kids in my backseat
and they left me in the parking lot
but the other kids were worse
and my bones may have well been ice,
the chill of storm reached in and cracked
me—all the will of skeleton with no
memory, all the will warranting no prayer
from the fake face of faith, instead
he put the fruit from the tree in my hand.

IX.

I dreamt of tornados with faces
calling to me from my basement
of glass. If the weather was my god,

I was holy—barometer alter
of cloud charts and inches of rain
offering no safety in knowledge.
The sky called to me in dark clouds;
the sky called to my children
with thunder. The Earth is a vengeful
mother and I have yet to say
that can't happen to me.

X.
I taught my daughters how to watch the sky

and I willed myself, too.

FIRST PUBLISHED IN *MAYDAY MAGAZINE*

Darren Demaree

* * *

EMILY AS SOMETIMES THE FOREST WANTS THE FIRE

It's always in the morning,
when the real quiet
kisses the bark ungently

& without bend or give,
a sturdy loneliness finds pause,
like a dancer in the tree-line

at sunrise, it will take great action
to resume our steps. Could it
be we need to run

from something, if only
to build a good lather? We can
call it dew, without panic.

FIRST PUBLISHED IN *CACTUS HEART*

Darren Demaree

* * *

EMILY AS WHERE WE SIGH

I am not sad
nor am I languishing
here with Emily.

I just needed to let go
of that air that briefly
was supporting me

until she returned.
Chest without gradient,
I am free to join us

as the hawk joins
the simple sky

with great mission.

FIRST PUBLISHED IN *DIAGRAM*

Lisa Dordal

* * *

AMANAT

On the night of December 16th, 2012,
a 23-year-old physiotherapy student
boarded a bus in New Delhi to return home
after watching the film Life of Pi.

The hyena kills the zebra,
then the orangutan.

The tiger kills the hyena.
And the boy survives.

Pi is an irrational number.
And a woman boards a bus.

If horses could draw,
they would draw one god

in the shape of a horse.
Oxen would draw many,

each with a body like their own.
And the bus is not really a bus.

The relationship
between the width of a circle

*

and its circumference
continues infinitely without

repeating. And Pi is a boy
who just wants to love

God. If dark matter could draw,
it would not draw itself.

The human intestine
is approximately five feet long.

Only five percent of hers
would remain. They would be called:

joyriders. The instrument used was
metal. The instrument used

was flesh. And the woman,
it was said, died peacefully.

FIRST PUBLISHED IN *CALYX*

Lisa Dordal

* * *

PRETTY MOON

Pretty moon, everyone said.
Before the noise, before

the fire. Two cars
and the cornfields idle

on either side. Like the eggs
of monkfish, emerging

a million at a time, knitted
into a gauzy shroud,

forty feet long, buoyant,
built for dispersal—the veil

between us and them,
thin. My cousin,

beautiful at sixteen,
dead at seventeen.

Pretty, pretty moon.
And me, at five, mouth open

*

not to a scream or even
to a word. Just taking in air,

quietly as a spider
entering a room.

FIRST PUBLISHED IN *ROVE POETRY*

Lisa Dordal

* * *

THIS IS PRAYING

For C., a resident
at Riverbend Maximum Security Institution

I hear a voice speaking
about a bird dragging its dark universe
of feathers across our yard,

and I realize it must be me
telling the boy how I carried its body
beyond the range of our dogs.

One eye, round as a coin,
fixing fear upon me, the other,
half shut. How the bird hauled

its body back into our yard,
dying with a will I could only
admire. Telling the boy

just to tell him something.
I can barely see his face
through the slot, eight inches

from the bottom of the door.
Pie-hole, they call it. I know
he cannot be cured of his crime.

*

But I can't help myself—
this language my body speaks
as I crouch, palms, knees

pressed against the prison floor.
Am I the bird?, the boy asks.
He is nineteen. He has an aunt,

a mother, both illiterate, both
a hundred miles away. No one knows why
they have stopped visiting.

I imagine his body, each Sunday,
learning again of their absence.
I imagine his organs, his bones

liquefying inside of his skin.
I imagine his eyes staring out
from his own gathered flesh.

It is three days before Christmas
and I have ten minutes to spread
something like joy. I think

of Vermeer, the woman in blue,
refusing to obey the physics
of light. I do not even know

the source of my own voice.
Am I the bird? There is a window
beyond the canvas but Vermeer

*

thinks a shadow will be
distracting. I tell him—the boy—
about a dream I'd had.

How my mind had been
like a living thing nailed down,
trembling with what ifs

and how comes. And then
these words: I hear you,
I hear you breathing. A sound

coming from within
and beyond. Not a voice, exactly.
More like a gentle pressing

of heat, the perfect distance
from flame, settling me immediately
into sleep. And now this voice

telling him: I hear him,
I hear him breathing, telling him:
it is a beautiful sound.

FIRST PUBLISHED IN *SOJOURNERS*

Susan Elbe

* * *

LISTENING TO RY COODER'S FEELIN' BAD BLUES

Slathered with well-bottom darkness, the stink
of this slide is my hanker, my haunt, my harrow

and a monkey moon loose in the night is
my rancor, my road-spent, my rising.

I should be inviting the angels on telephone poles
who beckon with pinwheel eyes,

but instead my fingers worry these rook-eyed
beads. They're my hammer and hesitation.

When it seems there's no light in this
dimming world, and only a small window

burns in a house too far, it's not those
angelic songs humming in wires

where I find my baggage, my bootstrap,
my backbone, but inside this gut-strung yowl.

*

Someone once told me, from the bottom
of a well, you can see stars in daylight.

FIRST PUBLISHED IN
Taos International Journal of Poetry and Art

Lara Georgieff

* * *

LE CHIEN

Napoleon, I love you shamefully.
With your pony hair, with your steel buckles,
with your faux medals that click as you walk.
I have pulled my hand from your mouth with a red cry:
blood on the snow, your mouth a sill of ivory,
my blood on the snow—yet I love you.

Who can say you don't deserve my allegiance?
Whole cities have failed us. People still jump when we pass by.

I raise my body and walk
with you when it's raining.
I have lain down on the floor with you
when you are sick.
I hold a jaune flower in my hand for you to smell.
Your eyes remain innocent.

You were sent to Corsica. They said you'd die
within three days
but who could not love you? You were behind bars.

Your clothing and medals were stripped from you;
injurieusement, they led you out to me,
sick, on a dirty rope. Innocemment, you begged
for oranges and buttercream.
My muscular-cheeked mafioso,

my boxy-headed boy,
you would speak only French.
I could just pronounce your name
but you smiled up at me without a trace
of the cunning I'd been warned about.

When I showed you where we'd live,
you wouldn't let me alone. You thought I'd leave you still,
slip down the drain like a fleece of soap.
You paused, blunt faced, portside the bed
afraid to come up, sure enough that I'd strike you.
But in the morning, rested, you craved
mayonnaise and cold water, thick white bread and dark coffee.

As for me, I didn't want to leave you alone again.
I heard you sobbing
from behind the front door
as I slipped my jailer's key into my coat.
I came home and my desk was thrown to the floor.
Your blood was everywhere.
You turned away in shame. I became yours.

Time showed that you were driven mad
by horses, by dogs, by men.
I'd find myself murmuring excuses for you in public
he's not well
Yet
how could I leave you now?
My bandy-legged triumphalist, your eyes would go lightless.

FIRST PUBLISHED IN *NARRATIVE*

Jeremy Glazier

* * *

IN THE AGE OF MONSANTO, VIRGIL RECONSIDERS
THE CONUNDRUM OF THE BEES

...amissis, ut fama, apibus morboque fameque...
Georgics, Book IV

This week has been hell on my allergies.
Everything bloomed at once. All that pollen
in the air: mountain laurel, tufts of cottonwood fallen
into snowy drifts. But wait—where are the bees?

Usually the backyard is bustling with the riot
of their constant, busy industries.
I snuffle, blow my nose, cough—and a sneeze
echoes through the purgatorial quiet.

How strange it feels when one's neighbors
start disappearing. Have they gone on leave?
Been victims of foul play—or pesticide?

I only know I miss their little labors,
which taught us, paradoxically, how to live
large, and well, and long, before they died.

FIRST PUBLISHED IN *CIMARRON REVIEW*

Matthew Guenette

* * *

INSIDE OUT

— *for Nate Pritts*

My mother's voice could jerk you inside out like a shirt.
          Then you'd be sorry
like when Steve stuck a snake in the fish tank.

          My mother's voice
could throw ice buckets over shower rods a mile away.
          Could kick

an attitude up and down Winter Street
          no matter how sweet it dressed.
Would daisy your ass

          and though she was small and wore sweaters
like a cheerleader
          my mother's voice could rise up taller than any backyard

all-star trash talk or whatever you tried to flip
          behind someone's back. It gave
side-effects like burning eyes.

          Rearranged faces like Picasso.
When my brother and I launched bottle rockets
          out our bedroom window

at the nutcase neighbors with the Reagan placards
        on their lawn, my mother's voice
was so rocket up the stairs

        even the cosmos paid attention. It could hear
you a thousand times in the graveyard
        smashing bottles or playing

with matches. It knew who gave who
        a Charlie horse, who ripped
who's boxers with a sky-high wedgie. It could see

        whose hand lifted
the five from her purse. It uncurled my brother's hair
        and I swear I saw it

in the headlights that night
        I played chicken with her Buick on Breakneck
Road, but when she had to come to the station

        at 2 a.m., had to listen
to some backseat-driver's lecture
        from an idiot cop about how to parent

before they turned me over,
        the scariest part was the ride home, an hour's
drive through a moonless dark, when she didn't say a word.

Matt Hart

* * *

THE FRIEND

—*for Nate Pritts*

The friend lives half in the grass
and half in the chocolate cake,
walks over to your house in the bashful light
of November, or the forceful light of summer.
You put your hand on her shoulder,
or you put your hand on his shoulder.
The friend is indefinite. You are both
so tired, no one ever notices the sleeping bags
inside you and under your eyes when you're talking
together about the glue of this life, the sticky
saturation of bodies into darkness. The friend's crisis
of faith about faith is unnerving in its power
to influence belief, not in or toward some other
higher power, but away from all power in the grass
or the lake with your hand on her shoulder, your hand
on his shoulder. You tell the friend the best things
you can imagine, and every single one of them has
already happened, so you recount them
of great necessity with nostalgic, atomic ferocity,
and one by one by one until many. The eggbirds whistle
the gargantuan trees. The noiserocks fall twisted
into each other's dreams, their colorful paratrooping,
their skinny dark jeans, little black walnuts

to the surface of this earth. You and the friend
remain twisted together, thinking your simultaneous
and inarticulate thoughts in physical lawlessness,
in chemical awkwardness. It is too much
to be so many different things at once. The friend
brings black hole candy to your lips, and jumping
off the rooftops of your city, the experience.
So much confusion—the several layers of exhaustion,
and being a friend with your hands in your pockets,
and the friend's hands in your pockets.
O bitter black walnuts of this parachuted earth!
O gongbirds and appleflocks! The friend
puts her hand on your shoulder. The friend
puts his hand on your shoulder. You find
a higher power when you look.

FIRST PUBLISHED IN *POETRY*

Matt Hart

* * *

from RADIANT ACTION

If you must, you must   Open your mouth
Let the light roll out   Ping-pong with books
Fire Fire Fire   Blinding lake water
Weird sisters, blood brothers   Dumb green hands
Come one come all to the wind-up spirit
The time unfolds with fist that shake,
lips that burst   The light is mine, it rolls along
The love is mine, too—is also mine   The Clash records
and the skateboards, the devil beside me, the meadow
beside me   The heavy water alphabet, the neighbor-
hood yea sayers of Cincinnati, all my friends' poems,
and my wife on arrival in the driveway after work, so
bewildered and beautiful, while I sit disheveled
and think about tomorrow, this porch, on this porch
The world skull is mine   The hoped-up, hopped-for future
is mine, the vanishment, the robots   But what's more
I belong to all of it   We are all of us inseparable
from creation and destruction, the floodlight
of darkness we emit in this life, moreover
the forces we attract, catch, miss   How do we
position ourselves to be our best   How do we
make all this hell into a heaven   Intractable heaven,
awash in the glare-gorgeous glare of it   O happy
new breath—not blood, not hornets, not venom,
not sonnets   I'm asking the questions, because I want

and need the answers   I wake up screaming
my whole throat to red   Today is the day
I'll attempt to make sense   My dumb green
heart is wide open

FIRST PUBLISHED IN *THE PROGRESSIVE*

Rebecca Hazelton

* * *

HOW WILLING A QUARRY

I told Michael I think it's possible to love
    more than one man.
If the first is a faithful
    retriever, and the second a snarling
ratcatcher, then the one will fetch your body
    from the frozen lake where the other
left it bloodied. He'll bring you back
    to yourself in his soft mouth,
damaging no part of you
    greater than already damaged.

Possible, but not well, Michael said,
    and gestured to his shirt front
where there was still a bit of blood.

How lovely we can laugh at this now, I thought,
    and I remembered then
that I was dreaming
    and it had been years
since he'd held my hand
    like this, so of course
his hand was gone, then of course
    he was gone.

*

But the lake was still there
    reflecting only itself
though the men had cut holes   to let the light in,
    and it seemed only natural
to drag myself across the ice again
    and wait to see what jaws would hold me.

FIRST PUBLISHED IN *32 POEMS*

Cynthia Marie Hoffman

∗ ∗ ∗

YOU WITH THE GETTING SHOT

It is a crisp autumn day when you get shot walking by the parking lot on your way to the lake. An arm goes up. A gun blows a hard kiss. You continue down the path, stepping around the acorns. You already got shot twice this morning. Always, you with the getting shot. You need to just let it pass. The lake goes on dragging the heavens this way and that. Your skin grows over the bullet. You sit at the shore with your back to the park pavilion where someone dismounts a bicycle and pulls out a gun. Over the years, your body has filled like a penny jar with bullets. Someone creeps among the trees. Your body heavy on the park bench. You watch clouds getting snarled in the rippling water, angels drowning in their tangled skirts. Someone's breathing down your back. There are no bones left in your body that aren't a clattering procession of bullets. You just need to rest for a bit. One after another, the white knots bob toward the shore but never fully arrive. Even if they did, even if they tumbled gasping at your feet in gauzy threads, you with your buckshot hands, your mind a shuddering animal hunkered down inside your skull, heaven help you, couldn't do a thing about it.

FIRST PUBLISHED IN

COLUMBIA: A JOURNAL OF LITERATURE AND ART

Katherine L. Holmes

* * *

THE OLD LADIES AT THE END OF THE WORLD

They situate their hindsight lawnchairs
to see perennials like a skyline
discoursing the longlost impulse.
The sparrows linger like stars
birdfeeders ford the bantered breeze
one outknits the gnats.

She gossips like the tied-down leaves
about loose felines and their progeny
and the sass who sold her food stamps.

Her sister hushed as cloud and hale
has walked on Sunday towards the casino
configuring sevens and blessings.

The daughter with the disease can see
the hope of downfalls all around
she laughs like a dirigible.

They hear the government like gypsies
they spread food for birds and strays
they impersonate the in-laws
calling a loner to their yard.

*

They sit through an evacuation
savoring it like someone else's forecast
the last to leave the area.

They only call at holidays
or when they can't move from the pillow
and the ambulance knows their doorstoop.

They might have stashed the gingerbread shingles
they left the workman like one last glimpse
and the aurora of a stained glass lamp
for those who passed and never saw
a Wedgewood couple on a pedestal
dancing to the Blue Danube.

FIRST PUBLISHED IN *THIN AIR MAGAZINE*

Lesley Jenike

* * *

THE CANON

That we'd seen a boy of twelve or thirteen riding a roan mare bareback through rye made no difference. We couldn't take the time to stop,

but if we had, we might've seen a whole village, its barn doors thrown open, all horses to market, each one young and sound. And in the air we'd smell the wholesome crush of dung and chimney smoke, and imagine the boy's other stock: a dapple grey colt he'll sell next month once it's broke. Stamping its hay, snuffling its grain, it smells the sweet tang of its own sweat. Sun through the stall's slats draws up the dust to which they—boy, roan, and grey—will go back.

Or we might've seen a high rise in Dublin where a boy tethered his horse to a stop sign. Next month he'll clatter it on blacktop down to Smithfield Market and sell it to a boy just like him: sweatpants, gym shoes, a yellow squirt gun. He belongs to a gang of kids whose ponies are called for rappers or favorite biscuit brands. They never need a saddle or bridle. What works is a fistful of mane, bully clubs tied to their belts with twine, mean-eyed looks, a wolf whistle. The market's cordoned streets will shine with piss and blood. Someone will be shot with a real gun and a horse will stagger from too little food onto cobblestone.

*

I'm waking up in the passenger seat and my father tells me how we nearly crashed, how he spun our rental's wheels toward a wall, dodging an oncoming tractor, a flock, a car, all while I was sleeping, my headphones on, and in my lap an upside down, half-read book wherein a boy refuses to grow up, is forced to sell his horse, then dies alone—in a city or on a dirt road, it makes no difference to anyone.

FIRST PUBLISHED IN *TUPELO QUARTERLY*

Lesley Jenike

* * *

PROOFS

In winter it's a lean snow that stacks itself. It's a dog of a snow that grows its bent for drift and howls to stick. Look:

a man in a cranberry hoodie on Finley Street says, "Leave it!" to his pit bull, and the pit bull leaves it.

On the causeway above the ravine, one schoolboy attempts to prove to his friend that a feather will fall faster than a stone. He's proven wrong, white goose feather in one hand, stone from the creek in the other, when on count of three, he lets them both go.

The stone of course plummets fastest while the feather—aping its past as a bird—hovers, flutters, glides and curls before it lands, so much later than the stone, it's nearly spring—and not yet spring.

A neighbor somewhere revs his motorbike, which sounds like a backfiring gun, and the congregations that remain scatter and take wing.

FIRST PUBLISHED IN *PASSAGES NORTH*

W. Todd Kaneko

* * *

READING COMPREHENSION 72: MAGNITUDE

We say rock and see it hurtle through space looking for a larger body to orbit until it settles into quarries of asteroids. We say paper and the redwoods understand the forest offers no safety so long as hatchets remain keen for bark. We say scissors and cut holes in the sky to manufacture new stars, in the ground to invent dinosaur bones. When we look close enough, everything looks imaginary the way we must look to alien telescopes—so small with our jagged perceptions of the universe. Our bodies feel connected to those shapes we make with our hands so we spread our fingers wide and say flowers, flowers, flowers. Forget that an explosion is a blossom of light.

Question: Which is bigger?

a) A supernova
b) The absence of desire
c) Rock

FIRST PUBLISHED IN *THIRD COAST*

W. Todd Kaneko

* * *

DAVID VON ERICH EXPLAINS THE RULES

> *I learned a lot about how to face these other guys*
> *who break rules [...] I never have been one*
> *that really likes rules because rules kind of hinder*
> *a man and hold him back. It's really better*
> *for me when I don't have rules.*
> —David Von Erich, professional wrestler

Rules are what separates a man
from the meat he eats. We can tangle
like beasts, you and me—get all thumb
and eye socket for the henhouse, all
shameless choke hold for the shambles.

When two men go at it all fireworks
and pistol whip, when two dudes
are done jawjacking and collide
all knuckles for claw in the boneyard,
the rules will blur into a flurry
of rabbit punches and country twang,
a spray of blood and flailing limbs.

It's not for love of skyscraper or handshake
or the Texas state flag that I live to be
the babyface. It's that the back burn is good
for the brush fire, that a man can't snuff out

a flame with his fingers without plunging
everyone into darkness. What makes a man
is not the blood staining his chaps,
not his will to go all monkey wrench
and brass knuckles in a feud. I can
pack a boot knife, tie a man down
with bull rope, pummel him with a cow
bell—I can be the bad guy, but we don't
always have to do things the easy way.

FIRST PUBLISHED IN *New South*

Sean Karns

* * *

THE SMOKE AND WE RISE

After Viewing Walker Evan's "Bethlehem, PA"

At the edge of town, a steel mill,
with smokestacks like skyscrapers, blows
smoke into the clouds—smoke that is for a moment
part of the clouds, then gone.

You never thought the smokestacks
would stop. You notice the town square
and houses that are still houses. Farther out of town,
farms still are farms, riverboats floating
on the river are still coming
and going.
There is a form to the town,
like the perfectly dug grave you stand by
in winter's mess.

There was a boy, you'll remember.
When your father left for work, you stood
at the living room window. You thought
a parade was going through town,
a procession of men walked
to work. In their hands, lunchboxes
swung like swings.

*

You are not that boy;
all sons leave their fathers.
You return to the ramshackle
harbor, twisted machinery
left to rust in the scrapyard, rotted
fields, the boatless river.
You are here in the cemetery,
abiding to tradition.
During the ceremony, snow-covered tombstones
fix you in their stare.

Seeing the bare oak tree,
you wonder what the cemetery
would look like in spring—the only
oak shading the small makers of
a small plot of land—enough land
to bury all who stayed. Maybe

wildflowers will grow against the fence,
blooming colorful waves around the cemetery.

You turn your shoulder from the town
slowly turning tombstone,
its histories in white ruin.

FIRST PUBLISHED IN *RATTLE*

Kathleen Kirk

* * *

PARALLEL LIVES

Parallel Life #1

In that house, where every bedroom
had its own tiny sink, the children
grew up brushing their teeth beautifully
before bed. We kept a collie in the fenced
back yard; she came in when she wanted,
and we walked her in the neighborhood
and let her run in the dog park at the beach.
The kids had to cross Clark to get to school
so I walked with them every morning
and afternoon until they were old enough.
My husband converted the triple garage
into his art studio, with plenty of ventilation.
I was a novelist. They made movies of my books.

Parallel Life #2

I never got out of the white apartment.
I'm there now, wishing the windows
weren't painted shut. There's nothing
on the walls. Across the way, on the fire
escape, a child leans too far over the rail.
Below, a woman is screaming no
but, yes, it's all happening.

Parallel Life #3

In another version of the too-white life
spiders take over the world.
I take photographs of their webs
and send them to art journals
until I am evicted but famous,
reconstructing it all in museums.

Parallel Life #4

I'm still in Ohio, in the brick place
with a stone porch on Buttles Avenue.
It's a long walk or an easy bike ride to work
at the university. I'm a librarian
with an interest in conservation
(not preservation. I hate microfilm.
Who doesn't?) We stage library dramas
(mostly comedies) after hours, and film them.
We get many hits on YouTube and lots
of government money. I let my hair
go white as vellum, white as the tough rag
paper of old newspapers from the Civil War.

Parallel Life #5

We divorced. Hard to say why. You kept
the three-flat. I kept the children.
One day they found you in the grandfathered
studio in the basement. You succumbed
to fumes—paint thinner in winter,

windows closed. They = the tenants,
not the children. I had to tell the children.
Even now, after so many years of telling them
who you were in pictures, you surprise them
by having a face. Eyes. A smile.

Parallel Life #6

This time, on one of your many swerves,
you fail to correct in time and we end
up in the redheaded ditch of November
prairie, in the rain. Understand me.
We are in present tense, briefly alive.
This is a dangerous game.

Parallel Life #7

We bought a small empty church
in a small empty town
and made it our home.
With all that stained glass light
and those high ceilings, it was easier to believe
in ourselves. You'd be amazed
how well this one turned out.

Parallel Life #8

I'm an extravert. I run for town council
and win. I'm married to an executive
at the insurance company headquartered in town.
A tree falls on the fence just the same.

Sometimes parallel lives do meet.
Notice the profusion of red and yellow leaves,
and many leaves still green. How the tree lies
perpendicular to its former self.

FIRST PUBLISHED IN *POETRY EAST*

Ted Kooser

* * *

APPLAUSE

for Maria Schneider

The woman who came to the concert
knowing the music by heart is the first
to applaud, instructing the rest of us
as to which of all the notes we've heard
was the very last, and the rest of us
fall in behind her, beginning to clap,
pretending we knew where it ended, too,
but were being polite by waiting a few
seconds longer, letting the beauty soak in,

and now we're ashamed to be the first
to stop, the first to turn to his overcoat,
crushed into the back of the seat. And now,
dear God, a man in the front row has leapt
to his feet and with a frenzy of clapping
much like a butterfly caught in a web
is shaming us into the Standing Ovation,
and then from the back comes a "Bravo!"
and then from one side and then another:

"Bravo! Bravo!" all of us now up and clapping
like crazy, clapping in mass hysteria,
hollering "Bravo!" and "Huzzah!" and other

goofy words we seldom find a use for,
wondering if we will ever get to go home,
the musicians beginning to wonder, too,
when to walk off, and whether they'll
have to come trooping back for an encore,
glancing around for direction while bowing

and bowing and bowing and bowing,
and now the conductor is stepping aside
with a swish of his tails and is pointing
at this one or that, calling for more,
feeling wonderfully good about himself
while all of us, on throbbing legs, would like
nothing more in this life than to discreetly
pluck our underwear out of our bottoms
and go home. But now, at last, it is ending

and the clapping is dying, one clap at a time,
the way a pan of popcorn quits popping,
and people are turning away, draping
their scarves around their necks, balancing
their programs on their upturned seats,
helping each other with their hats and coats
while the programs slide down and away
through the cracks at the backs of the seats,
never again to be pressed to our hearts.

FIRST PUBLISHED IN *RIVER STYX*

Leonard Kress

* * *

FISH

Why does everything come back to fish?
The time of year when the Maumee River
is flush with human jetties, casters, waist-deep
in the chill, arms like pistons, their manic Spring quest
for Walleye insatiable. The catch won't be served
for dinner, though—fear of poisoning their young.

Turn to the musings of Carl Jung
to make sense of synchronicity, his take on fish,
beginning with a human-aquatic figure that served
as an ancient alchemical inscription. On the river
bank he encountered a giant creature in its quest
to reach water, only to disappear in the deep.

That same day, he saw a patient, in deep
despair, recount terrifying dreams she had as a young
girl, and her whole adult life had become a quest
to make sense of those giant nightmare fish
that continued to haunt her. Later, at a cafe on the river,
he savoured freshly caught rainbow trout served

by a waiter named Fischel. In dreams, the archetype serves
as stand-in for libido or greed; or if it's deep
in the sea—unconscious urges; if it leaps out of a river
then fright or redemption. When I was young,

hard as I tried, I was never able to hook a fish.
Though I did set out on various quests,

or set forth (into the dark wood) to use language of quest,
to find the exact cause I was meant to serve.
I knew of the Grail and the aged, wounded Fisher
King from Weston's Ritual to Romance, I was deep
in The Psychology of Transference by Jung.
I kept my implacable sense that this river

(and all rivers like it) was the River
separating the living from the dead, the quest-
ioner from the question, and that while I was young,
I had to dive in, for everything's a matter of serving
or being served. And how to approach the deep
recessed pools of the incorporeal, commanding fish.

FIRST PUBLISHED IN *GULFSTREAM*

Michael Kriesel

* * *

ALEISTER CROWLEY LIPOGRAM

After Mark Zimmermann

I call a crow to steal its caw.
Soar air's aisles.
Eat scat.

A sorcerer's career is tears.
I salt a sea. Sow stars
across water's eye.

As Osiris, I see stars as tears.
As Isis, I see tears as stars.
As Crowley, I say we are stars.

As Eros, I call all.
Swallow Oscar. Wallow.
Lo, I attract Lolitas.

I start a Crowley sect:
writer, actor, satyr,
artist, liar, wastrel.

I retire to a twilit cell.
Create a tarot set.
Test astral laws.

*

Cast crystals at a cow.
I clear a way.
Stray.

FIRST PUBLISHED IN *NORTH AMERICAN REVIEW*

Michael Kriesel

* * *

INVISIBLE WOMAN QUITS FANTASTIC FOUR

Her life's a comic book.
Every month some megalomaniac in spandex
and a cape shows up to rule the world.

She's sick of fighting forty-story monsters named

Annihilus   Galactus   Fin Fang Foom

She decides to be an angel.

Leaves a note by the toaster, knowing Reed
will need its heat to see her invisible words,

remembering love letters penned in lemon juice
before cosmic rays aborted their orbit,

that fateful flight reducing them to adjectives:

Mr. Fantastic   The Thing

Human Torch   Invisible Woman

*

Shedding sea-blue spandex, an August breeze
stiffens her nipples. She turns invisible and leaves

to whisper *what's your power?*

in the ears of passing strangers.

FIRST PUBLISHED IN *THE PEDESTAL*

C. Kubasta

* * *

WORM SEASON

In early spring, the ground moves.
I take the dog out behind the garage, and she
freezes, lock-kneed, paws akimbo. The leaves
animate; if you're quiet, there's a muscular
rustling.

*

It's 1987; I'm eleven. I'm laying in the way-back of the van, reading
by flashlight. My two brothers are asleep, splayed across the bench
seat, and my parents are talking—quietly. I haven't been able to sleep.

In June, a girl-woman disappeared; they found her in the woods, chained
to a tree. In July, a schoolteacher disappeared: they found her in the
        woods. In
July, a mother of two disappeared—her kids at home, a basket of wet
laundry. They found her the next morning.

All I remember
were women chained to trees. I'd been reading
things I shouldn't.

They were talking, low. My father
said, "I told her they caught him." He said, "the cops think there was more
than one guy—"

"You didn't tell her that, did you?" asked my mother. "No," my father
said, "but it looks like a copycat."

*

I wake up with a sick stomach—agita. I dream I've been eating
sauerkraut. Each time you open the freezer, go outside
for a smoke, I'm awake, hoping you'll come to bed.

The worms are huge: big around as a finger, at least half a foot
long. Beware bare feet, or even flip-flops, sandals. If you stand
very still, leaves and skin whisk past.

It's the sound of the ice into the glass that does it. Open freezer, hand in
        ice
bin, two or three cubes percuss. (I don't need to listen
for the cupboard door, the sound of threaded plastic turning.) For the
first time, I think:

*

The story is that behind the garage was the outhouse for the original
homestead. Paradise.

The story is that murder one and three were unrelated; The story is

my father & mother worried about me. They told me a story, then undid
it, unknowingly.

*

The girl-woman's body was found in "the pines"—where the rural kids go to drink, and make out, and try to be adult. The worms work their way through a yardworth's of leaves each spring; a riot of writhing pink. This poem is a story too—only a story—. The danger of a final line is it becomes

the final line, a cage
of your own making. Tricky
stuff, this reverse
incarnation.

FIRST PUBLISHED IN *TINDERBOX POETRY JOURNAL*

Corey Van Landingham

* * *

PROCESSES FOR FORMATION

A man drew a map of the earth
and showed me how mountains are made:

fold and thrust, how plates collide
until one overtakes the other. He taught me
the long process of being subsumed.

When all I asked for
was to return to a time before there were words

for the types of weather.
To wake up in a different bed
under a different sky and not think Tornado Season.

I just want to be astonished.
Because, after awhile, I walked into rooms

thinking, How long is long enough
before I can leave.
The rivers were all the color

of old horses
too tired to run away.

*

Isn't the depth of desire
somewhere near drowning. When someone explains
how the world is formed

through its own deformation, how do I
not give him my only waist

to pull closer.
I walked into rooms like I could stitch
a feather into my palm and be

a hybrid kind of lover who is expected
to flee. And what if someone

took a pair of tweezers, worked it out.
What if someone
still had a little hope left inside her.

A little hope one could light up
            with a match.

FIRST PUBLISHED IN *THE JOURNAL*

Michael Levan

* * *

POET'S GUIDE TO THE HISTORY OF THE SECOND

You hear them on NPR, read them
on websites, store them for
cocktail parties and first dates.

Every second:
a hummingbird's wings flap 80 times.
Thunder rumbles 1,100 feet. Four to five people
are born; two die. At least 100,000 chemical reactions
fire in your brain. You lose
about three million red blood cells;
your bone marrow replaces them.
100,000 cubic feet of water pour
over Niagara Falls. The sun burns
nine million tons of gas.

Or if you counted a galaxy's stars,
one per second, you'd finish in 3,000 years.

But here's the truth:
the second, or the *second* division
of an hour by sixty, was born
in the late 16th Century, one hundred years
before measured accurately

*

until Earth's lopsided axis forced
its redefinition, then another
to the duration of 9,192,631,770 periods
of the radiation emitted by Caesium-133,

then again when this atomic measure
was found affected by altitude,
each second longer
in mountains than seashore.

So maybe hovering aside hibiscus
or sunset hyssop the bird flaps 81 times.
Maybe you lose three million and one cells,
or two-point-two people die.

You shouldn't be bothered,
but these are differences that keep
you staring into bedroom-dark.
Those numbers mean
to disorient you, almost as much
as leap-seconds added here and there,
which *did* make your fifteenth year
the longest of your life.

                    You've no choice
but to turn back abstraction.
Become a child again to make it equal
how long you could plash puddles
before lightning drove you inside.
Beg for second chance to run

in the rain, when everything
was simple as hide-and-seek's
One-Mississippi, two-Mississippi, three…

FIRST PUBLISHED IN *LUNCH TICKET*

Sandra Lindow

* * *

CINDERELLA BREAST

At the Palace, my paper gown
opens down the front,
exposing me to scrutiny
in a rapidly retreating anesthetized world:
"Why yes, Cinderella, you can have a life,"
Grand Vizier Medical said,
"but first we conquer that cancer:"
two lumps in my left breast,
entwining secret metastasis.
"Bibbety, bobbety, boo, make it go," I said.

But this sterile Kingdom
Is not Blue Fairy blessed:
No magic but the sticky-slick passing
of a surgeon's knife, mastectomy
and the beginnings of a promised
reconstruction, an alien
gazebo built under my skin,
normal saline added in,
cobble stone mockery of a breast
that presses heavily on my chest,
hampering my breathing
and making my heart race.
"Take it out," I said

*

Folklorists write
that the Woman's Journey
may start with a maiming,
far easier said on the page
than felt in the heart's center:
Heroism is lonely and hurts.
My old breast burned
toward inflagration. The fire is out,
but now that the parting's over,
I sleep unevenly on a cold hearth.

Losing more than a shiny shoe,
the ashes of health darken
my demeanor, and I see
a briared forest path twisting
into impenetrable dark.
The North Wind blows,
an ineffable animal howl.
I clench the hearth stones
awaiting the Chemical Bear
to slash and shred my quaking house.

FIRST PUBLISHED IN

ARCHAEOPTERYX: THE NEWMAN JOURNAL OF IDEAS

D. A. Lockhart

* * *

THIS CITY AT THE CROSSROADS

Knowing that you are measured
by all those thing that you aren't.
Neither butcher of the world nor
atavistic river port at the coal country
tip, instead you are known
for the quieter moments between,
hunting pigeons on war memorials,
major minor league baseball
and confetti in the quiet before
and after star-spangled parades.

For that, the question is about
simple notions of being, the bits
comprised of persistent anticipation,
the crushing whine of Indy cars
passing and then returning,
the inevitability of each return
amounting to the pleasure
taken from watching traffic
at high speed unable to escape
its mundane surroundings.

Maybe you are the leftovers
of those that couldn't be bothered
to finish their moving north

from the Commonwealth
to that metropolis on the lake.

All of it parts and pieces of one
sputtering chunk of an engine
with the clear belief that God
placed you on this prairie
where the glaciers rested
before retreating north, placed
you here to complete each lap
in good time and dream
of the sweet coolness of milk
drank through work-parched lips,
over a sun-cooked speedway
at the crossroads of a continent.

FIRST PUBLISHED IN *THE MACKINAC*

Karen Loeb

* * *

THE ENDS OF STORIES

At the finish of the meal, your father left. And that was that.

I led a reckless life, but when the accident happened, I reformed.

So I discovered that the bananas had to be really ripe.

The bouquet was a wet bathing suit moldering in a gym bag
tossed in the corner last month.

The lost earring with the green stone turned up years later
when they moved the dresser. She'd thrown out the matching one
a decade earlier.

The smell was a casserole forgotten on the counter. Something with tuna
and onions. It greeted them when they returned from vacation.

I plan to beat the odds and live forever, he declared.

The cat was hiding in the top drawer of the bureau, flattened
as thin as a comic book, eyes peering up, blinking, when we
finally found him.

Turned out it was a moth as big as a bat making those shadows on the cabin wall.

She went shopping for a jacket covered in feathers, just as it had appeared in her dream.

FIRST PUBLISHED IN *New Ohio Review*

Amit Majmudar

* * *

APOCALYPSE SHOPPING LIST

Lead-lined gonad-guards.
Lysol (radiation sickness causes killer runs).
Breadboxes, to bury stillbirths.
Flare guns, glue guns, gun guns.
Marijuana brownies for the burn units.
Ersatz shrouds (viz., bedsheets, towels, sails).
Triple-earwig-pincer Biohazard labels.
Fun Size Snickers Not Labeled for Individual Sale
But good to barter in a pinch.
Amputation pails.
Seeing-eye dogs bunker-kenneled in Kennebunkport, Maine,
To jog the flash-blind through uranium rain.
Astronaut ice cream for the bedbound.
Catheters (various calibers).
Lice combs to harvest protein.
Steri-strips.
Spike strips.
Benadryl, good for baby's colic or mommy's hives.
Teriyaki turkey jerky.
Paperback copies of Slaughterhouse-Five.
Bullhorns for the water rioters.
Firehoses for the riot police.
Wooden stakes, because you never know.

Four-ounce jars of Fleischmann's yeast.
Gallon jugs of Zen.
Rabbit traps, for the mice of the future.
Bear traps, for the men.

FIRST PUBLISHED IN *THE AWL*

Amit Majmudar

* * *

GROOMING

I shaved my face, and they called me doctor.
I showed up scruffy the next day, and they called me terrorist.
I grew out my beard, and they called me maharishi.
I left a goatee, and they called me Rushdie.
I cleaned it up into a mustache, and they called me fresh off the boat.
I got rid of the mustache, and they called me doctor again.
So tell me, I said, what brings you in today?
What is bothering you?
What keeps you up at night?

FIRST PUBLISHED IN *RIVER STYX*

Michael Marberry

* * *

WEEKLY APOLOGY

It's Sunday, so my favorite team is losing.
　　It's Sunday, so I cannot deny I love little

as much as I love this slow and systematic
　　destruction of Da Vinci's Vitruvian body:

the precision of a wideout's quick hot-read,
　　the fetishism inherent in four yards/carry,

and the headhunters' enthralling brutality.
　　Today, the hogmollies seem adept at pain,

and the quarterback seems more beautiful
　　because his spiral is the tightest of similes.

In the news, a man beats a woman in a box
　　and drags her down the hall, while another

tree-whips a baby like a disobedient horse,
　　and it's Sunday, and I'm celebrating violence.

If I'm a man, I am a man without a history
　　of cruelty, despite the tuggings of my nature.

*

Do we deserve our hurt? I can't answer that,
    though I feel I have known those deserving

of punishment and may be, myself, deserving.
    To harm someone and, in doing so, enforce

control and structure in our perpetual chaos
    must be alluring and wondrous and cathartic:

to learn what sound a body makes and where
    it leaks from. There is certainly that appeal,

which I can understand without condoning,
    which I know will be unpopular with you

(and rightfully so), as a conscientious reader
    expecting justice, which I cannot give you.

FIRST PUBLISHED IN *CRAB ORCHARD REVIEW*

Michael Marberry

* * *

LINEAGE

How can this word be robbed of its weight? I am

a white man and come from a long line of racists,

whom I love, abhorrently. My name: a question

on God, a woad hill with soon-to-be-blue fabrics.

I miss the days of language. (But there is no room

here for the kind and inside voices of literature—

only isocheims and kudzu lungs filled to the brim

with choke, various maladies.) I don't want to die.

I don't want to be sad anymore, even as the earth

reveals to me this ancient irony: No one survives

the future. We must lose the places we love most;

we cannot help it. And for all this, there is a quiet

*

resignation: perfect as water, its logarithmic ripples

or the sight of corolla growing in a deep, black bowl.

FIRST PUBLISHED IN *BIRMINGHAM POETRY REVIEW*

Matt Mauch

* * *

RECALL WHAT EMERSON SAID ABOUT LIFE AND

RECALL WHAT EMERSON SAID ABOUT LIFE AND
ALSO THAT 'ANSWER' IS TO 'HOMEWORK' AS
'DESTINATION' IS TO 'JOURNEY' BEFORE YOU
CHECK THE BOX THAT SAYS 'I'M READY TO BE
SOLVED' / To admit you have trod fields early mornings
for a wage, slouching towards the open hydrant of light,
a kind cash crop yourself, tending to a more naked kind,
feet beneath the secret canopy where the tiny talking
insects and rodents from all the old children's
storybooks are sipping gin, the sun a sci-fi madman
extracting sweat in large-dog licks from your forehead,
face, and nape, the sun wanting to taste, too, the salty
distillations of your loves-it-all life, dew penetrating
both sock and shoe, like the planet is a larger version of
you, like you are a smaller sun, is also to have to admit
to a field of equals signs, to your being on various sides
of various ones, and you're so sad that you have
accidentally destroyed already this morning so many
spider webs, walking with your jazz-boy's thighs,
planting and pivoting on your anticapitalist's heels,

wanting to lick again and again both the gift and the
ruins of the gift from everyone's feet, to be the brick and
fire in which this meal is cooked.

FIRST PUBLISHED IN *FORKLIFT, OHIO*

John McCarthy

* * *

DEFINITIONS OF BODY

Body 1. "Of Work": My mother did not—collected disability in the mail. The body is a paycheck inside an envelope held up to the light. 2. "Of Water": My mother was a river. Carried me into a gulf. When I was thirteen I dove into the trashcan to find the sunken orange bottles that resurfaced among eggshells and vegetables. She pulled herself under her own current. 3. "Of Bones": Her skull was a bag of voices. When she breathed, her ribcage moved like fingertips tapping together. Her teeth turned yellow, then white, then ghosts. She swallowed her ghosts, until she filled up with too many. 4. "Of Christ": Has risen. Revived at the hospital. The blood put back into her body with blood. The way I stood in the dark room and touched the IV hole to make sure she was real. 5. "Of Lies": Erased. She is not real. She has the intention to be a wraith. When she wakes and I ask how she is, my mother looks past me. 6. "Of Proof": The note I found which read, *I'm just so tired. I love you all tender. Goodnight.*

FIRST PUBLISHED IN *BEST NEW POETS 2015*

John McCarthy

* * *

SAMUEL'S EAR

My mother had two miscarriages
and I was born

with their voices inside my head, trapped
like nails in a glass cup,

pickled like sheep-children in mason jars,
raising their own kind out of their own kind,

a thought more than thought—thorns
burrowed under my skin, into my skull.

When they came out
of the orange light into yellow and white,

full of red and red everywhere—
the pain of childbirth having not birthed

never went away, my mother said.
Had they lived, at least a week,

there would be pictures
and soiled diapers, but my hands

*

and the hearing of innervations
drowned in womb-water slosh muffle

through me. Umbilicals attached
to nothing, wave like wheat stuck

in a cold wind in the middle of nowhere.
Voices beyond the voice—the language

of a dead child is the absence of crying.
To me it whispers, come to the edge,

that edge you stand on before you fall
out of your mother's legs and gasp,

gasp that thing you call life,
that thing of love and dust gathering

when no one's around.
I sense the two of them

on a shelf named memory,
named no one. I am Samuel's ear.

In the middle of the night
I wake up and haunt—

*

Eli, I call out to my father, asking
if it was him who called me,

asking what mutation made me
the father of my father's children.

FIRST PUBLISHED IN *RHINO POETRY*

Kevin McKelvey

* * *

FRIED EGG SANDWICH

Break two brown eggs into a bowl, pepper
them with black corns crushed in a peppermill,
pour eggs in the pan so yolks center.
More pepper. Medium flame, wait until
they look sweaty, then flip them over quick,
drop the bread slice in the toaster, get plate,
ready the butter knife, wait forty ticks,
butter the toast, give the egg to its fate:
toast folded in half, yellow yolk dripping
down fingers to the plate. After a bite,
use the sandwich like a squeegee, mopping
up that yolk. Perfect after a drunk night,
I have cooked one every day for a week—
your old favorite—and will until we speak.

FIRST PUBLISHED IN *EX., EX.: A MAGAZINE OF MIDWESTERN FOOD*

Michelle Menting

* * *

RESIDENCE TIME

Residence time (also called "lake retention time"
or "flushing time") refers to the calculated amount
of time water spends in a particular lake.
It is also the amount of time it takes
for a substance, once introduced into the water,
to finally flow out of the lake again.

My sister tells us the true story
  about when she was hit by a truck.
This isn't a tragedy, she says, but a flash
  of true fiction. And she tells us
how she went running, how she took off
  that day hours before dawn, before any of us
pulled back our blankets and stretched.
  Already she covered eight miles of back roads
bordered by pine trees before the Chevy Half Ton
  or Ram Jeep Hummer little monster
of a truck driven by a smaller monster hit her,
  clocked her good, made her spin and kiss the tar.
She recalls the backstory, how once she babysat
  the driver when he was five: how then he dug
his fingers into the grass, how then he pulled
  fistfuls of sod and stuffed the sprigs, roots and all,
into his mouth. How then he thumbed his nose
  at the year-round kids who came over for cookies

and Transformers. How his coordination
  was all pumps and smacks, even then,
like an overgrown baby who knows manipulation.
  He was cute, she says, how he waddled
with precision even at five, his legs so accustomed
  to a bellyful of beef and not of poached venison.
That summer in our northern town,
  where everyone knew everyone's golden retrievers,
my sister, back from college, watched these children
  of part-time residents for full-time pay.
Fast-forward eleven years. We can tell stories that way,
  she says fifteen years later while we sit around the campfire,
all of us home reuniting near the lake.
  But then she finishes her telling, not the story
just her talking about it, with the smack of that truck,
  how it bruised her thigh, how she felt hot air
after her left hip bounced off the blacktop pavement.
  But she kept her head held high, she says,
like when you stretch your neck to keep from drowning.
  She noticed the early sun. She foreshadowed its rising.

FIRST PUBLISHED IN *Ocean State Review*

Mary Meriam

* * *

THE NATURAL WORLD

Body   ocean   body of blossoms   touch me
Sea of certainty   am I dreaming now   or
Lilac drowning   throw me a lifeline   sometime
        Save me   undress me

Then affection   then in the night   the deeper
After-rain   when grasses and leaves are singing
Notes of such sweet scent that we hurry   gladly
        Into the hidden

Now the stars   the sky   distant planets   pull me
Now the forest whistles   hello!   water!
Body blossom blooming   alone   alone   so
        Touch me   and touch me

FIRST PUBLISHED IN CIMARRON REVIEW

Pamela Miller

* * *

THIS MUCH WE KNOW

All disasters begin inside tiny padlocked boxes.
The periodic table is dissolving before our eyes.
Therefore, the Taj Mahal will become a hotel for ghosts.

All women secretly want to be Theodore Roosevelt.
But none would be caught dead in this centipede bikini.
Therefore, who am I to dip my fingers in boiling oil?

No cathedral of exhaustion has spires that point sideways.
An imploding neutron star can't dance on the head of a godsend.
Therefore, we must all till the futile fields of sleet.

All human beings compare themselves to battlefields.
All fallen warriors are reborn as shards of silence.
No man is an island, but some women are.
Consequently, our hearts turn so easily into ladders.
Therefore, the world politely refuses to end.

FIRST PUBLISHED IN *OLENTANGY REVIEW*

Tracy Mishkin

* * *

END OF THE WORLD, PART II

I am hiking with my lively dying friend, holding hands. She lets go to roll down a hill. At the bottom, she shakes off dirt, jogs back to me. The tumors, which she counts every night, are starting to rise like silos under her skin. Yesterday she let me feel one on her thigh. Her death is real now, a womb-baby that's started kicking. No due date, but she says she won't see ninety, like her mother did. Or her birthday in November. It's crisp and nice for winter now, but I tell her the weatherman has forecast one hundred twenty inches of snow tomorrow night. "That's a lot of snow," she says. "I probably won't see you again." I am so tired of walking through these shadows. She says, "Let's take a nap." We lie down together in the flat, brown grass that's doing the best it can.

FIRST PUBLISHED IN *LITTLE PATUXENT REVIEW*

Julia Anna Morrison

* * *

SUGAR

The winter moon turns on again. I want to lick
ice off the windowpanes.
I haven't left the house today. On this bed
I will become a mother, a cannibal in a wet bra,
eating my placenta like a sugar cube.
Soon my stomachs will empty their baskets of
stars on the ceiling. How hungry will I get.
Every flutter I only imagined, the baby
an angel going back to being an angel—born
from the defrosted sea in a bright blue coat.

FIRST PUBLISHED IN *The Journal*

CJ Muchhala

* * *

LET US PRAISE BROWN

for it eases us into the stark season,
for it is the color of earth
worms, the color of dung
and of dirt which generates
the green we celebrate
and the popple's silvery
leaves shivering in the wind,
and without which nothing
can live.

Let us praise brown
for it is the color of homespun
poverty which joyful Francis wore,
for it is the raiment of eagles,
of summer rabbits and of the wren
which makes a joyous noise at Matins,
and let us praise brown for it is the color
of acorns, raining from oak trees
sharp against roof and road,
sustaining the bear's long sleep,
and of pine cones lying
in wait for fire to melt their hearts
into green.

Let us praise brown
for it is the color and richly
pleasing smell of coffee
beans roasting which belies
their bitter black brew,
and let us praise the tasteful
brown shade begotten of cream
for otherwise we would taste
in every mugful and many times daily
our lives. So also let us praise brown
for it is the color of the bitter cacao bean
which belies its brown sweetness sung
in many tongues: chocolate, *choclad,*
suklaa, sjokolade, kokoleka,
for it is bliss, for without it love
might die.

Let us praise brown for its mute
simplicity, for its unobtrusiveness,
for its meekness and humility,
and for the self-effacing way it dims
neon lights, street lights, house lights, billboard lights,
until the city beds down in brown-out and the stars
revive.

FIRST PUBLISHED IN *NIMROD INTERNATIONAL JOURNAL*

Richard Newman

* * *

THE OS AFTER THE SILENCE

> "The rest is silence. O, o, o, o. [Dies]"
> — *Hamlet, V, ii*, variant from first folio

I've pried from my garden an O-shaped bone,
three fingers long and wide,
worm-licked and white as moon.
Picked up—the loam that held it crumbles away.
Put to my eye—I view the world through death.

Overheard one morning, a friend moans
from the downstairs couch, her sorrow
stifled with cushions as she sobbed herself
awake—or back to sleep—dampening
my fake velvet with dozens of little Os.

The morning after a crash, we neighbor kids
snared a tire from ditchweeds and bloodied gems
of glass and dribbled it down the road, great thwacks
against the asphalt, a bouncing rolling O
with nowhere to go but over hills of soy.

Chorus heaps on chorus, and after the last
chord cuts off the cascade, a young woman's
voice warbles out, frail O hoping to join
once more the refrain, the bobbing sea of song,
but no—her lips an O of pleasure and then,

*

at finding herself alone, no longer lost
in music but found by us, oh no of shame,
dark O covered by a hand but echoing
in our mind's ears longer than any song,
longer than laughter, her O for more, her O
to merge, her O to be lost on waves of O.

FIRST PUBLISHED IN *BOULEVARD*

Elizabeth O'Brien

* * *

WHAT IT WAS LIKE BEING A TANAGER

Remember what it was like being a tanager
flying a jigjag kaleidoscope of sunspot, cornfields,
snuffed cloud, pond scum, parked yellow bus lots
were runes spelling dirty jokes below remember
bombing the squares? The beaches filching bread
crusts and grubs and you had the sweetest chortle
rup-chirup you ruffed my wings nipped my neck
we were ragtag getaway kids wearing our mothers'
feathers, ducking vultures on low afternoons
perching our stubby butts in a row hooting
jimmying sweets from the trees teasing
the poults and fledglings three or five of us in it
for the scolding.
We hung all day around the telephone pole
waiting for the buds to pop in the trees for
the rest of the gang to come flocking once I
ate the head of a rusty nail by mistake I
got stuck in an attic you screamed at the
window *hurry she's come with the broom.*
We gobbled seeds and bugs anything
we got our beaks on anything
we wrested from each other our appetite
was endless remember the hawks, the bullycats,
slapping our faces into plate glass windows
drunk on gnats scrambling up and away

cawing, you bent the tip of your wing,
I lost a toe. Anything set us off
we were plumey soft. Our beaks
were stout but our wings were bright
we were growing the trees were growing
the telephone pole seemed to be growing
it was all cricket and sing and South, go South,
everything gogo and riproar, rolling in dirt
the twitch of grass, shift of sky, the song
we sang remember it went fly fly away, fly.

FIRST PUBLISHED IN *Sakura Review*

Eva Olsgard

* * *

DEARFREYJA://

It snows.
It is snowing.

Snowflakes break against brick.
The courtyard is a well of wind.
The air outside is as cool and distant
as the television they tend like a fire
in the flat across from mine.

The city beaches are covered in snow,
white dunes crested in black.
It is so sad to watch brown clumps cling
to the undersides of municipal busses.

At night I play a keyboard without strings.
Plastic keys creak like bones.

It snows.
The snow is falling, completing
a silence that will never be complete.

All down your road this time of year
pine trees bow to the ground in humility
beneath a mantle of snow. You ski
the parted river between two shores.

*

In the forest you ski all day,
cutting white from white.
Frost pales your cheeks.
You grow a beard of icicles.

You ski uphill leaving tracks like fish bones
to be scattered by the next solitary skier.
On the evening trail, you find your way home.

It snows.
The sun is rising. The Snow is Dancing
plays on a German radio next door.

I want to come home to the birches,
their pink flesh hidden beneath the white

FIRST PUBLISHED IN *PINYON REVIEW*

Deonte Osayande

* * *

VIRTUALLY DEADLY

They didn't know I was black
the first time I got called a nigger. We played
video games online, the one place

where black boys fire guns
without becoming instant monsters. While winning
the match I didn't realize what fires waited

inside of us boys until I made the victory shot
on the kid on the other end of the internet, releasing the poison
from his viperous tongue. I didn't have a mic

when I was online, which is to say I didn't have a voice
to hurt him with any power my words could possess,
which is to say I found myself blacker than I knew

as unheard as I always had been. Minutes
later came the second time, from a couple
of teammates, as a term of endearment, a thanks

for covering their backs, acknowledgments
of a good job listening to orders. I'm certain
they didn't know I was black, didn't know

*

how insulted I was, but I'm also certain they wouldn't have
cared so long as I continued to follow orders. At that time,
I was one of the best at my favorite online shooting games,

which is to say pulling triggers no question, following
orders, more comfortable with real and fictional death
than my own blackness. When confronted with the story

of Joan of Arc, I cried like the Catholic schoolboy I was.
Let the news report another victim of violence who looked like me
and I wouldn't flinch. Today I've been listening:

I have veterans for friends. I know how quickly our country martyrs us,
how it burns us at the stake when returning from war, instant monsters
if owning guns without ever targeting other black bodies

while following orders. I know how loud the unheard cries
against the violence are. I know how comfortably snakes sleep
at night, aware of our deaths. I know this isn't a game.

FIRST PUBLISHED IN *MOBIUS: THE JOURNAL FOR SOCIAL CHANGE*

Donna Pucciani

* * *

WHAT MY FATHER TAUGHT ME

The word "feign" means "pretend,"
as a boxer in the ring,
though my father preferred
tennis to the fights.

When I was twelve
we'd go for walks on River Road.
He'd invented a kind of skip,
a hiccup in the pace. He'd signal "now,"
and together in a blink
we would soft-shoe once,
laughing together but feigning
that nothing had occurred,
our eyes on the road ahead.

Sometimes I would play
the old mahogany upright while he,
mimicking Ezio Pinza in South Pacific,
sang "Younger than Springtime"
over my shoulder, whistling
the notes he couldn't reach.

I learned from him to camouflage
mother's affair with gin.
We'd tell the neighbors

she had a touch of flu. I would be
as respectable in my navy school blazer
as he in his Brooks Brothers suit.

He was my fighter, my magician,
my master of pretense, and the day
mother took too many aspirin,
he could do anything for me
except make me disappear.

FIRST PUBLISHED IN *PULSAR WEBZINE*

Divya Rajan

* * *

L AS IN LABELING

There are freedoms only a crumpled brown bag that once
Cradled a Manhattan sashimi in its folds, now meandering
At the crux of I-294, would acknowledge.
Freedom to glide and scrape by cars, without fear
Of resurrecting most onerously as an upturned fable. Now
That's the kind of iniquity she came to enjoy the most
As the newest inhabitant of this pristine space.
Vijayan, a vague synesthete, a writer of sorts, arrived here
Much prior to her, his feet dripping with all the salty liquid
Of redemption, of stale morphine. Who better to work on translating
Khasakkinte Ithihasam, he winced piously. He wasn't being
An idle provocateur, I guarantee you that.
Seriously? That sounded a bit con-mannish even to me.
Who the fuck still lived in the old world? She nodded
As if it was old news to her. Being agreeable was a virtue
She'd carried forth. Her brothers had long shed loitering leanings
Settling for elitist discernments towards ala carte movies
That played non- stop in the background as they
Chomped noisily over political science, other urgent topics
Somewhat like what she did on social media, her
Grey cells indistinguishable from moss. They made filter coffee in the
        mornings
In a rustic coal set kettle the old fashioned way, decoction
Stronger than the strongest espresso, mahogany chair on the porch
Creaking, crushing leaves. Bird droppings shared names
With siblings, unlike in the other world. Plethargic

Wasn't their last names. I explained to her, that wasn't the case.

That she was morbid and whole in this green planet, with me.

She didn't hear or bother to listen, spread suntan lotion

On her tooth brush, scrubbed teeth till they were semi- brown.

I said, "Do you realize what you just did? Look at your brown teeth."

She smiled, "Silly, that's an overdose of iron supplements.

I ain't no nutmeg." Another time, she smeared baba ghanoush

Over her hair and left a post- it for me, with instructions to clean the
pillowcase

In a mouthful of a mixture of chicken broth and extract of St John's Wort.

The psychotherapist listened to her patiently and remarked,

Only a lousy caregiver would leave assorted cans unlabeled.

FIRST PUBLISHED IN *SUNFLOWER COLLECTIVE*

Julian Randall

* * *

AND THEN GRIEF BECAME THE WINTER

and February became a parade of tight
throats and all the bottles went from
brown to empty while the wind slaked
its thirst for exposed skin   until
we just started figuring the sun was
a myth because we'd seen so many
rising and falling   again
that surely this was just another name
we had not forgotten yet February was
a broken mirror a mass of bodies
the white noise of everywhere
was fists in pockets and everything
brown   emptying   suddenly
I had too many hands debatably
too many names and everywhere
was slaking its thirst for exposed skin
and the room had been emptying
for as long as any of us could
remember and I started playing
at Prometheus kept smuggling
different names with me all of them
brown fit to slake my thirst or
remind me what the sun tasted like

FIRST PUBLISHED IN *THE MADISON REVIEW*

Rita Mae Reese

* * *

ON THE PROBLEMS OF EMPATHY

1
Twice a year the orphans come.
Like Job's children, pawns in a bet
made with the Devil.

2
You and your mother watch
from the porch as Father Whiskey's car
rolls up the long dirt drive.
The orphans inside ignore the fields,
the cows, the pond, the patch of woods.

3
When you were younger,
you begged for a brother,
or even a sister.

4
What should you say to an orphan?
You think of your mother's
habitual prelude to sympathy:
"There's nothing easier
than burying other people's children, but..."
The orphans are beyond sympathy.

5

Sympathy being one of the problems.
How far does it go?
Not quite to the horizon.
Not even to the trees beyond the pond.

6

The orphans, their still-breathing,
lye- and cabbage-smelling bodies,
are also a problem.

7

Father Whiskey with his lazy eye
thinks a good Catholic family
with only one child is both
problem and solution.

8

One eye looks at your mother.
The other looks at God
looking at you.

9

Sympathy requires action, or at least words;
empathy is a private affair,
which is nevertheless a basis for community.
However the distinctions are imprecise and need further work.

10

Father Whiskey sees God looking at you as if
—if you believed in the Creed, the Holy Ghost,
and all that he has tried to tell you,
if you could even look a statue
of Mary in the eye—
then you could reach out a hand,
lay it on this boy's scrubbed forehead,
make him your brother.

11

Later, in college, in a winter of mind and place,
you will read Edith Stein's
On the Problem of Empathy.
Now though she is of no help to you.

12

You stand on the front porch
and wait for the miracle
to begin in your shoulder
and travel down through your fingertips,
the way you've heard lightning
tries to escape the body.

13

In a few months there will be different orphans.
Then the time comes but no orphans.

14

Years later, in a city where you can't speak
the language, you will pass a woman
sitting on the pavement, a burnt-out shell
of a woman holding an infant. The infant is sleeping,
on his head a robin's-egg-blue bonnet, spotless.

15

Your problem is you feel too much, or not at all.

16

Their grown bodies move past you.

FIRST PUBLISHED IN *RATTLE*

Andrew Ruzkowski

* * *

I'M SORRY IF YOU CAN'T UNDERSTAND ME BUT I TRIED

I'm sorry if you can't understand me but I tried
I know myself in small chips & fragments
each time I move from one room to the next
& to the next   There are many common things around
like papers doorknobs milk butter & eggs
The rhythm in the floorboards slowly melts
Outside the sun shines but is not felt

We talk about gardens & how the juniper felt
against your skin   I collect sharp fragments
of porcelain & pretend they are ancient candles melting
in my hand   Perhaps they mark what happens next
or what has already happened   I once stole eggs
from a kildeer as she shouted around & around

her nest among the rocks   We sing in the round
together sometimes   Sometimes at bars I ruin felt
pool tables because I'm drunk & clumsy & full of pickled eggs
which you hate   They disgust you just like my fragmented
speech   You say how can I be so dumb   Next
time you'll leave me with my eggs & patty melts

We tell ourselves this place is not worth the lamentations that melt
in our mouths like sky   Don't say that stupid shit around
me   you say   when I speak & claim to know what happens
next

between us   It is so relaxing crafting things with patient sounding
names   I feel
small plants on my fingertips like dandelion sumac & linden   What   I
meant
to say is that I'd love to cook you eggs

to prove my worth as a lover   according to the French
I'd beg
if I thought it would help   or simply watch the butter melt
I want to know your synapses & their jumping thoughts
My body is spent
after each time you fuck me   My body bound
& breaking without a care from you   Swollen from repeated belt
lashings & bleeding from the buckleIs this the sex

I dreamed of as a boy   When sex was filial & reeked & I was
undressed
slowly   carefully   as his hands fumbled between my
legs
Sometimes I feel like a prize or some exotic pelt
Sometimes I dream of stale beer & the way he smelled
Again   you say   go back to those birds you found
& the rocks too & the trees & the flowers with names like Tilia argentum

The roof leaks & erodes & you are hell-bent on what comes next
Do you feel honor bound to prop me up or hang me on a peg
To save me or leave me with just a belt around my neck saying you've
helped

FIRST PUBLISHED IN *PERMAFROST*

Max Schleicher

* * *

ANOTHER BEGINNING

In the beginning, all the world was America.
Sharp rainy seasons, skies scaled with mica.
Bright wind. Brittle lakes. The air would flinch
with lightning and a flex of nameless birds
fell to the grass, tumbling in wadded cinders.
Their taste taught migration to plain herds.
Animals devoured each other, hacked clotted fur
growing the claws and shoulders of those they ate.
In the beginning, action wasn't separate
from fear. There was one language: swollen branch
and stifled breathing. Even as the rain ended,
the small remnant fears beaded each leaf crimp.
Crowded in pools, we were born. Our necks pinned,
we stared up, afraid we were the beginning
and could not be killed without being forgiven.

FIRST PUBLISHED IN *ZÓCALO PUBLIC SQUARE*

Maggie Smith

* * *

WHERE HONEY COMES FROM

When my daughter drizzles gold
on her breakfast toast, I remind her

she's seen the bee men in our tree,
casting smoke like a spell until

the swarm thrums itself to sleep.
She's seen them wipe the air clean

with smoke, the way a hand smudges
chalk from a slate, erasing danger

written there, as if smoke revises
the story of the air until each page

reads never fear, never fear. Honey
is in the hive, forbidden lantern

lit on the inside, where it must be dark,
where it must always be. Honey

is sweetness and fear. I think
the bees have learned to embroider,

*

to stitch the sky with warnings
untouched by smoke. Buzzing

is the sound of bees perforating the air,
as if pulling thread through over

and over, though the thread too is air.

FIRST PUBLISHED IN *VIRGINIA QUARTERLY REVIEW*

Maggie Smith

* * *

READING THE TRAIN BOOK, I THINK OF LISA

In the board book there is a train, not a train
but a picture of a train on thick cardboard pages
my son fumbles to turn. In the book with a spine
gummed soft, there is no car parked beside the tracks
and no black-haired woman standing by the car
not parked beside the tracks. In the book
there is a train, each car its own color, one car
heaped high with coal, not coal but a drawing of coal.
See the engine, the neat cloud of steam above it,
not steam at all, and the engineer in his striped cap
smiling in the little window, not a window.
In the book there is no black-haired woman
on the tracks, not tracks. I am holding my son
who is holding the train book and waiting
for me to sing the long, happy sound, not happy
but a warning, doubled and doubled again.

FIRST PUBLISHED IN THE *KENYON REVIEW ONLINE*

Emily Stoddard

* * *

PRESERVATION PRINCIPLES

I once laid out my collarbone as a tripwire,
convinced that exposure might be a kind of compromise.

*

    I ate my own voice box for fear
that it would reveal too much—

Mute then, but the mind of the heart still assembled
a violent vocabulary.

    Memory is never so easily swallowed.

*

    I ate your pain like a rock unpolished—

        Cracked open my wrists so you could see I am real,
           human like you. But your hands are soft.

    You don't take to calluses.

           And your teeth—
           Untrained for rock.

*

Now I drag my tongue like a rotting fish through salt.

Where were you while I was dismantling myself?

Here is my body, open and uncured.

You were never going to stitch me
back together.

FIRST PUBLISHED IN *MENACING HEDGE*

Bruce Taylor

* * *

THE POEM IN PROGRESS

The way an almost autumn morning
comes to south facing houses
on the far side of the river,
slow along a low bank sculpted
by an August afternoon,

from a window where you always sit
a view from the second story,
the slightly bigger picture
of the smallness of your life.

Time passing not so much
as staying and settling,
the dead float of an old boat
adrift in the leaves, the crawl

of the shadow of a hoe aslant
the garage wall, a guilty thing
surprised by the slowness of its shame.

FIRST PUBLISHED IN *THE LAKE*

Jessica Thompson

* * *

A SEASON OF TICKS AND HARD RAIN

Suppose they are standing in a root cellar
that has lost its ceiling. Suppose

they are looking for relics: blue
glass vessels she will fill with the harvest.

Suppose they have lived through
a season of ticks and hard rain.

Suppose their laughter is trapped
within stones. Suppose he will leave her,

only she doesn't know yet
and won't until after

the fields are cut. Suppose it is so—
one month later,

when the rafters cry out
under the weight of tobacco—

she strips and hangs herself in the barn.

FIRST PUBLISHED IN *KUDZU*

James Tolan

* * *

LEAVING HOME

for James Wright

Eight years of Reagan, and our fathers slouched,
hollow as robbed graves,
atop their bar stools daily. Union jobs long gone,
they were men of a dying age, chewing
the well-gnawed bones of how good they had it,
when they hated the shift boss
and the shift, when they pulled too much overtime
at Anchor Hocking, Johns Manville, Abbott Labs.

What became of our once proud fathers—
their flinty surrender to what they were
abandoned to remain in our industrial town—
one among the reasons
we fled to what our haggard adolescence
could imagine of escape, of lives decent and full
of something more than beer and hope confounded.

Grubby, middling, next-door neighbors to white trash,
we drove late nights packed
like livestock into our fathers' wheezing rides
to scoop the loop and spy on those we envied

*

for their happiness and ease
as they poured into places a man might lift a glass
to more than a life he never meant to love.

FIRST PUBLISHED IN *I-70 REVIEW*

* * *

AND NO SPIDERS WERE HARMED

1.

Sister Therese writes in a letter that she
has a spider on her pile of books,
wants to know if I ever wrote about them.
How to confess that I, who people call
bug man, get the willies around them.

Some, anyway, the ones with the fat,
fat bodies, or those that scuttle fast
across the log I sit on, or the kind
that hang so still I think (hope) (pray)
they might be dead, but I know are merely
waiting, patient as death, as only spiders can.

And then there are the ones that take on
the colors of flowers they sit in,
match the sun-yellow coreopsis
or the pale purple violet where they
ambush bees, snatch them as they sip
the nectar. Man, that does not seem fair.

2.

During WWII, people raised spiders,
even black widows, harvested

the silk strands (30 times thinner
than human hair), and used them
to make

          b

          o

          m

          b

          |

c r o s s —   — h a i r s

          |

          s

          i

          g

          h

          t

3.

An arachnophobe, he says, yet
Nicholas Godleya, fashion designer,
orchestrated the creation of a cape
woven from spider silk.

It has a mystical, ephemeral quality, just like a spider's web...

One point two million golden orb spiders
caught on Madagascar, their silk
harvested. Afterward the spiders were
released unharmed, back into the wild.

4.

I am fascinated by them,
but still frightened of them ...
I am slowly trying to overcome it,
but it hasn't stopped.

5.

It hasn't stopped,
                        this punch-to-the-gut

                              feeling, this I-really-am-
mortal

            feeling, this queasy
                        unbalanced-ness,

when my friend's obituary

                  sprang

out of the screen
                              at me

while searching for his address on the Web.

6.

The air over the lake by the monastery shimmers on this
clear fall day. One could almost say *perfect day* if there
was such a thing. I hesitate to even write the word

gossamer. Some will say *cliché.* But there are hundreds of
gossamer strands drifting over the lake. Each one a prism.
Yes, they were glinting like rainbows. They looked like
music. Each filament ferried an unseen spider from one
place to another. How can we see the wispy strands so
much thinner than human hair but not see the rider?
This is how the wingless travel.

7.

A Japanese scientist spun thousands of strands of spider silk
into a set of violin strings. The brown recluse, a venomous
spider, is also called a *fiddleback.* Musicians tested the strings
on a 1720 Gillot Stradivari. They said the silk created a new music.
I imagine a whole arachnid orchestra. A spider sonata.
A fiddle that bites. Music that doesn't let you go.

8.

After the last organ notes faded
the kids in the pew in front of us
sang and played itsy-bitsy spider
with their hands.

FIRST PUBLISHED IN *THE MADISON REVIEW*

Steve Tomasko

* * *

YOU SAID I SHOULD WRITE MORE LOVE POEMS AND

I said, I'm sorry, but I've been thinking about
sloths. Well, actually, the moths that live
on sloths. Nestle into their fur, take the slow,
slow ride through the rain forest. Once a week
the sloth descends to the forest floor. Defecates.
Female moths leap off; lay their eggs on the fresh
feces; jump back on. Their caterpillars nourish
themselves on the fetid feast, metamorphose
into moths, fly up into the canopy to find
their own sloths. They prefer the three-toed
over the two-toed. Who can figure attraction?
The algae-covered sloth fur is the only home
the sloth moths know. The only place they live.
I know it's a Darwinian thing but *fidelity*
comes to mind. Commitment. Patience.
The world writes love poems all the time.

FIRST PUBLISHED IN *THE FIDDLEHEAD*

Lisa Vihos

* * *

LESSONS AT THE CHECK POINT

> *Please be advised that snow globes are not allowed*
> *through the security check point.*
> —LaGuardia Airport sign

Is this because of the snow? Or because of the little houses
that nestle inside the snow?

I imagine it is because of the liquid
and the potential to inject an explosive

through the dome of the glass. Evil is inserted every day
into our minds, under our skin, through the iCloud,

through layers of data that shred the ozone
(an ozone held together by scotch tape, chicken wire

and American Idol.) One day, someone picks us up,
shakes us, and all hell breaks loose. Worlds collide.

The very equilibrium we once believed in,
cast aside by a wave of the hand. While some God,

somewhere, waits at a check point, watching
for the terrorist in each of us,

*

wary of small things, like six ounce jars
of olive spread, beard trimming scissors, and yes,

snow globes. These things tucked in between the socks
and underwear, waiting to destroy us.

FIRST PUBLISHED IN *WISCONSIN PEOPLE & IDEAS*

Claire Wahmanholm

* * *

LULLABY

The loon's eye is a carmine moon.

Is a Mars.　　　　Stirs

in its orbit as the wind stirs the lake's loose face

into haloes whose

arcs swell against each other until they disappear　　　or

are blown into new diagrams,　　　battle plans, lessons

for a war that cannot

reach us here,　　in this pocket of pine forest I tuck you into.

Hush.　　Thrush

and snail, moth and bat,　　are reconciled, held

in the same dark mouth.
　　　　　　　　　When you ask for a story, I

hum the names of lunar seas—*Nubium, Imbrium*

*

Vaporum, Crisium—

which are not seas, whose

water is a dark silt,   basalt

shallows empty enough to look like

a face.
          When you ask, I sing about the hole in the bottom of the sea,

a lesson in

microscopy, in vertigo.   *O*

little eye,   little eye,   there's always a further layer,

an infinite splitting,   a tunneling.   Sung,

this is

just soft enough to sleep by.
                    The loon's eye drifts on the lake like

a broken beacon

above a slow drain. Like a body orbiting a black hole. Wool

spun from cloud to thread to the pupil of a needle's eye. *Hush-a-bye,*

*

hush-a-bye,   *I*

didn't mean to make you cry. Lake is lake, loon is loon; the eye

was only ever an eye.
                        A red-throated

morning yawns the sky.

FIRST PUBLISHED IN *WAXWING*

John Walser

* * *

LOVE POEM

after Robert Bly

When we are in love, we love the hole in the muffler
that vibrates our neighbor's car into our living rooms,
and the seagulls that colonize the roof of the abandoned grocery store
   at the end of the block,
and the motionless June air that will crack open, flood spill the gutters,
swirl into the half-leaf-clogged storm grate.
Years ago I watched an old man broom handle poke water.
I watched a city bus push a tide up the street toward him.
When we are in love, we love that old man's hands, his ankle soaked
   trousers,
and the city bus and all the faces looking out of its windows
   at him teetering.

FIRST PUBLISHED IN *THE PINCH*

Timothy Walsh

* * *

NORTHWOODS METAMORPHOSES

Imagine the leaves on the trees were basically the same
except that each leaf weighed, say, five pounds.
Imagine the terror each autumn would bring—
leaves crashing down on roofs, landing with a thud,
    smashing sidewalks, cracking heads, squashing squirrels,
obliterating windshields, falling like cannon shot
    into rivers, streams, and lakes.
No gentle fluttering of weightless, butterfly-like shapes
    wafting and lilting in the wind,
but solid wedges plunking down like chunks of cement.
Imagine the now-pleasant chore of raking leaves—how we'd
    strain to lift each five-pound leaf into a wagon
or wheelbarrow, stack them like bricks along the street
    for city crews to come and get.

Imagine if the five-pound leaves on the trees
    were otherwise the same
but were made of something like meat—
choice steaks falling from the sky—
maples tasting of beef, oaks of pork—
collecting the leaves to marinate and season,
    broiled to perfection.
Imagine that these falling, five-pound leaves
were what sustained us—
how we'd ache for the coming of fall, mouth watering

at the thought,
watching the changing leaves as we watch ripening
      apples or raspberries.

Imagine if the five-pound, meat-like leaves of the trees
      were basically the same,
except that they came alive as they fell,
sprouting legs and feet, snouts and faces
      as they plummeted to earth,
scurrying off as they hit the ground to hide
      from the legions of blaze-orange hunters
and their barking, leaf-sniffing dogs.
Imagine the glorious October leaf-hunting season,
the forests alive with fleet-footed leaves,
      wily as raccoons, playful as otters,
the distant pop of guns, the smoke of wistful campfires,
hunters tracking catalpa, ash, hickory,
      freezers full of leaf-mulch sausage.

Now imagine that the five-pound, meat-like leaves of the trees
      that came alive as they fell
were basically the same—
basically the same as, say, your own hands,
      pointed and veined,
attached to branch-like arms and trunk-like torso,
your feet tethered to deep subterranean roots,
yourself standing tall in the breeze under
      a benevolent blue sky,
your clothes woven of gnarled bark,

*

birds settling on your branches,
nesting in your hair.

There. Now imagine.

FIRST PUBLISHED IN *STONEBOAT*

Tori Grant Welhouse

* * *

CANOE

His first smile is a canoe.
He has no idea.
The smell of his neck is a long journey.

He makes me think of lilypads.
I am thoroughly familiar with his gunwales.
Help me.

The paddle drips in his lap.
My hands callous.
We do not have a rhythm.

Pelicans plunge.
He is anxious about whitewater.
Waves slap the waterline.

He is careless about rocks.
We can't help but float backwards.
Paddle already!

The river ripples viridian.
He can't see past the thwart.
I will not change places.

FIRST PUBLISHED IN *MINERVA RISING*

Mark Williams

* * *

FRACTALS

A cloud is made of billows upon billows upon
billows that look like clouds.
As you come closer to a cloud, you get not
something smooth but irregularities
on a smaller scale.
— Benoit Mandelbrot

July 4, 1973. I'm the guy driving the blue Ford Pinto
with the flammable hatchback and white vinyl top
which will give me cleaning fits for the next ten years
before it turns gray and I sell the car to a woman who will claim,
"A Pinto saved my life!"
          Lucky for me,
she will be broadsided and not rear-ended in her combustible engine
soon after my buddy Bob (that's him in the passenger seat)
and I celebrate college graduation with this trip to Maine.

That's Indiana in the background.

*

You can tell it's Indiana by the number of cars with Indiana plates.
Otherwise, it looks a lot like Illinois:
corn, soybeans, Howard Johnson's.

*

I've seen every highway in the United States by now, and they all look alike to me.

    —Loretta Lynn

In 1975, Benoit Mandelbrot will notice
that if you break certain geometric shapes into pieces,
the little pieces look pretty much like the big shape.
And if you break the little pieces into littler pieces,
the littler pieces look pretty much like the big shape.

                               And so
                    on . . .
He'll call the shape a *fractal*.

The road from St. Louis through Ohio is a fractal.
But I don't know that yet. It's still 1973.
Benoit is at IBM, busy figuring,
as Bob and I exit I-70 into a small Ohio town that—
with the exception of the parade we suddenly find ourselves
wedged in—
looks like all the other Illinois, Indiana, and Ohio towns we have
exited into.

This time Bob is driving.
That's us behind the fire truck.

And that's the melody from "American Pie"
carried haltingly by the trombone section
in the marching band behind us.

On May 19, 1979, I will stagger through mile twenty-six
and step onto a quarter-mile cinder track
with about fifteen other straggling runners:
                    a kind of sad parade.

    "Ah, ha, ha, ha, stayin' alive, stayin' alive,"

                                    a cruel loudspeaker
will sing
as I limp across the finish line into a canvas recovery tent,
where I will notice a slender, fair-haired girl
recovering from her run with the aid of a cigarette.

The beautiful girl will not notice me.

But in this parade the Buckeye girls who line the street
can't seem to get enough of Bob and me, cheering wildly,
wildly waving as we pass—
the two of us doing our best parade waves
through the open windows of my Pinto, in return.

Clouds, snowflakes, certain animal-coloration patterns
                    (a leopard comes to mind),
broccoli, cauliflower:
            fractals all.

Lungs, pulmonary vessels. Galaxies!

That's Bob and me on top of Cadillac Mountain,

stuffed with wild blueberries we've consumed along the trail.
We're looking at Maine's coastline.
In a few years I'll learn it's a fractal, too,
along with ocean waves parading toward shore.

Lightning bolts. Also fractals.

But I won't be thinking about that either—
after we descend Cadillac Mountain and the rain
and lightning start for real
and we realize no way will our pathetic little tent protect us
like a cozy bar in Bar Harbor and a beautiful girl or two
who can't wait to take us to their cozy home
from a *bah* in *Bah Hahba* would.

What a magnificent coastline!

*

Here are some things I remember from that night:

1.) driving into Bar Harbor in a downpour;
2.) naming lobsters (Larry, Louie, Lonnie, et cetera)
   swimming in a restaurant tank;
3.) watching paramedics revive a cook who inhaled
   while priming a propane cook stove with a rubber straw;
4.) eating lobster (Larry) for the first time;
5.) deciding never to name another meal;
6.) walking into a bar on Mount Desert Street
   and seeing a slender, fair-haired girl smoking a cigarette—alone;
7.) noticing the beautiful girl did not notice me;

8.) noticing the Bunyanesque, black-and-red plaid figure
     who suddenly eclipsed the bar's door frame
     did notice Bob and me sitting at a table
     with his slender, fair-haired girlfriend, Uta—
     Uta having already described the ahgument
     she and Little Jack had earlier that day;
9.) slow dancing with Uta to "A Whiter Shade of Pale"—
     with Little Jack's permission;
10.) a lava lamp.

*

Here are some lines from a poem called "Relax," by Ellen Bass:

Your parents will die.
No matter how many vitamins you take,
how much Pilates, you'll lose your keys,
your hair, and your memory.

And then:

Your wallet will be stolen, you'll get fat,
slip on the bathroom tiles in a foreign hotel
and crack your hip.

Except for the hotel part, Ellen has me pegged.

Could we all be little pieces?

Chips off the Old Block?

*

Here are some fairly accurate lines from a bar in Bar Harbor:

Little Jack: One time th' snow was so frickin' deep
          I stubbed my toe on th' top of a telephone pole!

Me: No kidding.

Little Jack: One time we used a puhtato for a football!

Bob: No kidding.

Uta: These guys need a place to stay tonight.

Little Jack: One time I walked into a bah
          and found two guys hittin' on my girlfriend.
          So I gave 'em a choice. They could buy me beeyah
          for th' rest a th' night—and I'd give 'em a place to stay—
          or we could go outside and settle up anathah way! Ayuh.

Me: Oh bartender.

*

Dear Uta,

I'm the guy who was driving the blue Ford Pinto
with the white vinyl top, the guy who followed
you and Little Jack home in what he called a "wicked pissah"
forty years ago. The other guy was Bob.
I hope you and Little Jack are having good lives.

(Perhaps there are Littler Jacks and/or Small Jills.)
More than likely your life has seemed a succession of small parades.
Chances are your parents have died and you've lost your keys.
Uta, does the world sometimes look like it's slipped
on the bathroom tiles in a foreign hotel
and cracked into 7,173,302,544 angry little pieces? Anyway,
I just wish everyone could get along as well today
as the four of us did that night.
We skipped the light fandango, didn't we, Uta? After all,
we want the same things: a nice meal, a drink or two, some music,
and someone to share the meal, the drinks, and music with.
Plus a dry roof above our heads. You might say
we are irregularities on a smaller scale.

A belated thanks, Uta. My best to you and Little Jack.
And if you missed something from your kitchen that next morning,
please forgive me.

Though it was Bob's idea.

*

Sunrise: July 8, 1973. That's Bob and me

waking up on Little Jack and Uta's screened porch.
In Yorktown Heights, New York, for all I know
Benoit Mandelbrot is measuring broccoli florets in his sleep.
But in our sleeping bags, Bob and I are figuring the odds of a sober Little
Jack
appreciating us as much on his porch this morning
as he did in his favorite bah last night.

*

Predictably, we rise.
Sadly, we sneak into the kitchen and snatch an orange.
In my Pinto, Bob peels the orange and asks me to slow down
so he can toss the rind into the harbor.
"For Larry's cousins," Bob says.

Bob breaks the orange in half.
We break our halves into littler pieces,
pop them, one by one, into our mouths
                    and drive away.

*

July 10, 1973. That's my Pinto pulling out of Stuckey's,
where Bob and I bought four Pecan Log Rolls
and two packages of Pecan Divinity—
to repay our parents for college educations.
Bob will marry Jeannine, a French tennis player.
I'll marry DeeGee, the fair-haired runner
who will finally notice me and complete my parade.

But for now, that's Pennsylvania in the background. From a distance,
it's hard to say which guy is Bob and which is me.

FIRST PUBLISHED IN THE SOUTHERN REVIEW

Hanif Willis-Abdurraqib

* * *

AFTER THE CAMERAS LEAVE, IN THREE PARTS

I. The Ghost Of The Author's Mother Performs
An Autopsy On The Freshly Hollow City

They listenin' to the wrong music again, child. When the smoke rises and sinks its teeth into the meat of another dark sky, people always wanna act like "Mississippi Goddam" was the only song Nina Simone blessed the earth with. Probably 'cuz if you sit on the floor with a record player in a room quiet as a dirt-lined casket, you can hear the black bones cracking right there underneath the piano keys. You can taste another man's blood climbing slow up the back of your throat. Feel the water cannons start to press through the walls and soak your feet. Might even be able to see the one hundred snapped necks hanging from the edge of the needle when Nina sings "Lord have mercy on this land of mine..."

And if that don't carry you to the front lines of any city trynna paint its streets with your blood, lord knows nothin' will.

But didn't nobody sing "Sinnerman" like Nina. Didn't no one else cast that spell right. The confessional ain't no good if nobody confessin'. Nina, though. Let every note of "Sinnerman" hunt for a wicked tongue. Forced it to lift its secrets to the warm air. You play that song over what's left of any scorched city, and watch. All them white men gonna start runnin' from they homes, crying the names of what haunts them into their bloody palms. 'Til the middle of the street splits wide open. Swallows them whole. I know. It ain't gonna bring nobody's dead child back. But I ain't seen "Mississippi Goddam" do nothin' 'cept flood a house of black bodies 'til they washed up in the heat of a city, bloated and dying.

My daddy never taught me to swim.

I ain't never take my babies to the water.

II. *The Convenience Store's Broken Glass Speaks*

have they stopped / whispering the dead thing's name yet? / I was promised / the brick's heavy kiss / would spread me thin / over where they killed the boy / and then I would become the new / dead thing / to grow ripe in every mouth / I would become the thing they remember / in the summer / I show up to the party late / and loud / I drink the house into a desert / I keep the whole world thirsty / I stay after everyone else leaves / I keep you awake until the sun comes / I crumble the body / I leave the jagged void / I part the whole country / I Moses the Midwest / come children / walk through my toothed bed / to the other shore / we don't talk about death over here / we don't speak its name / we don't name leaving / we wake up to a new day / we don't think of who didn't / look at my body / stretched out on this holy ground / like I'm almost human / like I'm almost worth grieving / and why not? / people have to mourn the shatter / of anything that they can / look into / and see how alive / they still are

III. *What Is Left of "Sinnerman," After The Fire*

Oh,

      sinner

*

run

sinner   run

run

Don't you see

this

bleedin' river

Don't you see   the devil

waitin'

FIRST PUBLISHED IN *PEN AMERICAN*

Hanif Willis-Abdurraqib

* * *

ALL OF THE BLACK BOYS FINALLY STOPPED
PACKING SWITCHBLADES

To punk shows ever since the summer of '98 when danny went into the
pit and got his front teeth divorced from the rest of his mouth by the fist
of some white boy from the side of town
where no one buries a body that came into the world after they did and
no one ever has to swallow
their own blood and pray that it will keep them fed until morning
so danny told us that he was going to
go home with someone's teeth even if they weren't the ones that he came
here with
because how many things have we boys had ripped from our mouths and
never replaced by anyone?
how much of our language has been pulled over the tongues of everyone
but us?
reparations were sought in dark alleys with a blade sharp enough to scare
a jaw open and a prayer out of a sinner's body which explains how the
white boy wept
and called his father's name when being pressed
into the brick with danny's foot against his neck while we watched until
danny finally let the boy
go and we ran back out east towards our homes and maybe
it was the way the rain howled or maybe where
we come from we see everything drowning in red anyway
or maybe there is no other way to explain the haste with which I make my
pockets barren before leaving the house

even today

or why my wife needs a bigger purse to carry such weight for the both of us

but when the police came for us that night

we did not hear a sound until danny's blade fell out his pocket and the bullets that followed

because I guess anything can be a gun if the darkness surrounding it is hungry enough

or at least that's what I've been told when

the bodies of black boys thrash against what

little life they have left tethering them to the earth and isn't that what we've always been fed? that it is just like the nighttime

to rename everything that moves

into a monster?

FIRST PUBLISHED IN *WINTER TANGERINE*

Tess Wilson

* * *

KANSAS CITY INTERNATIONAL

When you leave
if you leave
you will wade
the margarine
pools of Topeka
night lights.

When you leave
if you leave
you will breathe
the Kansas breeze
and you will bird
every summer.

When you leave
if you leave
you will blink
the flicker of fields
whipping by on
Wyandotte Road.

When you leave
if you leave
you will bleed
the City of Fountains

and quench your
autumn thirst.

When you leave
if you leave
you will sleep
the blue cold
of limestone.

FIRST PUBLISHED IN *NEAT MAGAZINE*

Sarah Ann Winn

* * *

FLOATS

July fourth. Baseball's on the radio,
a steady hum from the garage
outlasts the locusts for an inning.

Tonight the fireworks will
splay and fall over the lake,
but now in the lull after picnic,

a little work sweetens the languor.
A hymn of mending to be done,
perpetual hum in work clothes

at tool benches. Hum of a.m. radio,
hum of a job well done. Grinding
a machine file, a drill and electric saw job.

A thirst for work, ground down waterless.
A quenchable need to shape for use.
Thirst to be finished, to restart, to righten.

Salt of drive. Of worn hammers
ready to drive home. The well-driven nail,
head flush with board. The carpenter's tools

*

love the carpenter at work. In the shade,
a yellow mug full of root beer waits,
slowly forms a ring of sweat on the workbench.

The ice cubes melt away, ebbing as tasked.
The machine needs to be tended. Runs all afternoon.
Salt added to sweet drone of memory.

When the ice cream is ready,
we may scoop it into mugs for floats,
sweetness brought to sweetness,

sip then sneak a dribble of salt
from the side of the metal churn.
Root, it speaks of origins.

FIRST PUBLISHED IN *SAN PEDRO RIVER REVIEW*

Sarah Ann Winn

* * *

HOW TO FOLD A DREAM

You have to think first of the breakables.
The four mockingbirds growing smaller
on receding fence posts
must be stacked one inside the other
like nesting dolls. Wrap their song in a cyan silk scarf.
Place it in the smallest.
It must be tucked in carefully.

Take down Venus.
Pack it separately—it's fragile,
wish laden.
Store the thunder in your laughter,
and eat the red orange sunset while it's still ripe.

Fold the juniper-freckled fields
in the velvet peridot your grandmother
draped over her couch.
Follow the creases like a map.
The riverbeds are readable as
the lines in your palm.

Rearrange the constellations.
Move Orion closer to Diana.
Locked in a hunter's embrace,
each will keep forever in the Gulf Stream,

their reflection moving on the water
like a skiff made of stars.

Don't surrender that last kiss to waking.
Drop it in your pocket.
Take it out when people aren't watching.
Admire its crimson petals,
the thrilling yellow-jacket bump of desire.

FIRST PUBLISHED IN *Sugared Water*

David Winter

* * *

RE: (NO SUBJECT)

I picture him fondly on all fours,
eating scraps off the floor, his skin

washed of its scars by the bad light
he liked. Unmuzzled, he used to say,

We are having a romance. Now he's gone
and written all my little cruelties out

of our pulp novel past. His latest letter
is a lovely ruse, but it is not a knife

I care to use. No, it's a slow ember
I cradle in throat's depth. He wrote,

and asked if it was wrong to write.
I breathe his smoke into the night.

FIRST PUBLISHED IN *THE OFFING*

David Winter

* * *

FANTASY

What are you thinking, I ask, and he says,
I think you're leaving me, and I say, *That*

is manipulative. We're not talking about love
but power play, and where it doesn't end.

I keep thinking you'll stay, Reader, if I leave
out the parts he calls *ponderous*. But I need you

to know every highway between Columbus
and Brooklyn, the Greyhound's fluorescent

dawn, and how many times we've each written
this ending. We never did need a safe word

so much as a cartography of the triggers
and havens we make of each other's clavicles.

He knows when I say *No* I often mean *Harder*,
and you're learning that in fantasies I confess

*

only to what I haven't done. That's why I left
out the argument's interior, every imagined

crime—and that's why I say *No* one last time
when we both understand the answer is *yes*.

FIRST PUBLISHED IN *FORKLIFT, OHIO*

Scott Woods

* * *

CLARKSDALE

blackness scouring the source of darkness
blinded by courteous light in every corner
an international front has taken the beach
we are surrounded by good intentions

the juke joint host described as surly
in the visitor's guide is not pretending
people used to dance to this music
right after the moan
spread over a lie of land so flat you could
run your fingers across its washboard fields
and tune a thousand souls

stranger in a foreign homeland
all eyes on us, taking the measure
of the black folks without instruments,
come to see the blues zoo
please feed the animals
watching us watching them watching the blues
like everybody forgot how to listen and drink
at the same time
can feel the diary entry I am becoming:
saw a black man smiling at a blues show last night
knew he wasn't a local
tapped his toes in all the right spots

*

staying in a sharecropper cabin
refurbished for that genuine blues experience
even the spiders are imported
want to take every board and throw it in my trunk
build it over again where it belongs
burn it to the dark meat
likely the ground

somewhere in the world right now
there is a song playing
that will not end for a thousand years
it is not a blues song
it is a machine song
it is a system song
it is a caprice, an exercise, a trick
it is flight and fancy and ha ha ha
it is bowls and chimes and drones
all things you can play low and slow
into the grave
a song you meditate
that you travel many miles to hear
in very few places on earth
it will play for a thousand years
after all the black people have gone
and somehow for whatever reason
we will call that the blues

FIRST PUBLISHED IN *Urban Contemporary History Month*

CONTRIBUTOR
BIOGRAPHIES

SUSAN AIZENBERG is the author of three poetry collections: *Quiet City* (BkMk Press 2015); *Muse* (Crab Orchard Poetry Series 2002); and *Peru in Take Three: 2/AGNI New Poets Series* (Graywolf Press 1997) and co-editor with Erin Belieu of *The Extraordinary Tide: New Poetry by American Women* (Columbia University Press 2001). Her awards include a Crab Orchard Poetry Series Award, the Nebraska Book Award for Poetry and Virginia Commonwealth University's Levis Prize for *Muse*, a Distinguished Artist Fellowship from the Nebraska Arts Council, and the Mari Sandoz Award from the Nebraska Library Association.

MARILYN ANNUCCI was born and raised in New England, but she has made her home in Madison, Wisconsin, for nearly twenty years and teaches in the Department of Languages and Literatures at the University of Wisconsin-Whitewater.

FATIMAH ASGHAR is a nationally touring poet, photographer and performer. She created Bosnia and Herzegovina's first Spoken Word Poetry group, REFLEKS, while on a Fulbright studying theater in post-violent contexts. Her work has appeared or is forthcoming in *POETRY Magazine*, PEN Poetry Series, *The Paris-American*, *The Margins*, and *Gulf Coast*. She is a Kundiman Fellow and a member of the Dark Noise Collective. Her chapbook *After* was released on Yes Yes Books fall of 2015.

SAYURI AYERS is a native of Columbus, Ohio. Her work can be found in the *Santa Clara Review*, *FreezeRay Poetry*, *Waccamaw Journal*, *Relief*, *Pudding Magazine*, and others. Her chapbook, *Radish Legs, Duck Feet*, was released in 2017 by Green Bottle Press.

JULIE BABCOCK was born, raised, and still lives in the Midwest. She is a Pushcart Prize nominee and recipient of grants and fellowships from the Indiana Arts Commission and the Vermont Studio Center. She is the author of *Autoplay* (MG Press, 2014) and her poetry appears in various journals and anthologies including *Hayden's Ferry Review, PANK, Weave,* and *Feast!* (Black Lawrence Press). She is a lecturer at University of Michigan.

MELISSA BARRETT's poems have recently appeared in *Narrative, Gulf Coast, Web Conjunctions,* and *Best New Poets 2013.* She is the recipient of an Ohio Arts Council Individual Excellence Award, a *Tin House* writer's scholarship, and a Galway Kinnell Scholarship from Squaw Valley's Community of Writers.

MICHAEL BAZZETT's poems have appeared in *Ploughshares, Massachusetts Review, Pleiades, 32 Poems, Sixth Finch,* and *Copper Nickel.* He is the author of the chapbook *The Imaginary City* (OW! Arts, 2012). His first full-length collection, *You Must Remember This* (Milkweed 2014), was the winner of the Lindquist & Vennum Prize for Poetry.

JEFFREY BEAN is Associate Professor of English/Creative Writing at Central Michigan University. He is author of the poetry collection *Diminished Fifth* (WordTech) and the chapbooks *Girl Reading a Letter at an Open Window* (Southeast Missouri State University Press) and *The Voyeur's Litany* (Anabiosis Press). His second full-length poetry collection, *Woman Putting on Pearls,* won the 2016 Red Mountain Prize for Poetry and was published in 2017 by Red Mountain Press. His poems have been featured on *The Writer's Almanac,* in the *2014 New Poetry from the Midwest* anthology, and in Garrison Keillor's anthology, *Good Poems, American Places.* Recent poems have appeared in *Antioch Review, Missouri Review, Poet Lore, Willow Springs, Smartish Pace, Crab Orchard*

Review, and *River Styx*, among other journals. He can be found online at www.jeffreybeanpoet.com.

ROY BENTLEY has authored four books of poetry, including *Starlight Taxi* (Lynx House, 2013). His poems have appeared in *The Southern Review, Shenandoah, Pleiades, Prairie Schooner*, and *North American Review*—and in the anthologies *New Poetry from the Midwest* and *Every River on Earth*. He has been awarded fellowships from the NEA and the arts councils of Ohio and Florida. His newest manuscript, *Nosferatu in Florida*, was a finalist for the 2015 Moon City Review Poetry Prize and the 2015 New American Press Poetry Prize prior to being accepted by the University of Arkansis Press under the title *Walking with Eve in the Loved City* (2018).

MONICA BERLIN's work has appeared or is forthcoming in *Cimarron Review, Kenyon Review, december, Water~Stone Review, Cincinnati Review, Crazyhorse, Salt Hill, Passages North, Bennington Review, Kudzu House Quarterly, Hayden's Ferry Review, Grist, Hobart, TriQuarterly, Ninth Letter, DIAGRAM, Third Coast, RHINO*, and *Missouri Review*, among many others. Her first book, *No Shape Bends the River So Long*, a collaborative collection of poems with Beth Marzoni, was awarded the 2013 New Measure Poetry Prize, judged by Carolyn Forché, and was published in early 2015 by Free Verse Editions at Parlor Press. An associate professor of English at Knox College, in Galesburg, Illinois, Berlin teaches nonfiction, fiction, and poetry, and serves as Associate Director of the Program in Creative Writing and Chair of the Department of English.

TOM BOSWELL is a poet, freelance journalist and community organizer residing in Evansville, Wisconsin. His poetry has appeared in *Rattle, Poet Lore, The Potomac Review, The Dos Passos Review, Two Thirds North* and other journals. His manuscript, *Midwestern Heart*, won the 2011 Codhill Poetry Chapbook Award and was published by Codhill Press in March, 2012. He also won first prize in the 2012 Poetry Port contest sponsored by Bookstore Number 1 in Sarasota, Florida. In 2006, he was awarded a Fishtrap Fellowship for poetry judged by Luis Alberto Urrea. He was also recently designated an International Publication Prize Winner in the *Atlanta Review* annual contest and won first prize for poetry in the Prose & Poetry Contest for Emerging Writers sponsored by *Glass Mountain* and judged by Tony Hoagland.

JAN BOTTIGLIERI grew up in suburban Chicago and now lives in Schaumburg, IL. She is a managing editor for the literary annual *RHINO* and received her MFA in Poetry from Pacific University. Jan's poems have appeared in *Court Green*, *DIAGRAM*, *Willow Springs*, and elsewhere, and she has led workshops in poetry for the Northwest Cultural Council. She is the author of the chapbook *Where Gravity Pools the Sugar* and the full-length poetry collection *Alloy*. When she's not writing poetry she enjoys baking, movies, and building pillow forts.

TRACI BRIMHALL won Second Place in *Narrative*'s Seventh Annual Poetry Contest. She is the author of *Our Lady of the Ruins*, selected for the 2011 Barnard Women Poets Prize, and Rookery, winner of the 2009 Crab Orchard Series in Poetry First Book Award. Her poems have appeared in *Best American Poetry 2013* and *2014*. Born in Little Falls, Minnesota, she earned a PhD from Western Michigan University.

JOSHUA BUTTS' hometown is Jackson, OH. He has earned degrees in English from The Ohio State University and The University of Cincinnati. He teaches at the Columbus College of Art and Design where he also serves as Head of English and Philosophy. His work has recently appeared or is forthcoming in *Spoon River Poetry Review*, *Birmingham Poetry*

Review, *Tampa Review*, and *Burnside Review*. His first poetry collection, *New to the Lost Coast*, was published in 2015 by Gold Wake Press.

KAI CARLSON-WEE is a Jones Lecturer in poetry at Stanford University. A former Wallace Stegner Fellow, he received a BA in English from the University of Minnesota and an MFA in poetry from the University of Wisconsin-Madison. Carlson-Wee lives in San Francisco.

SARAH CARSON was born in Flint, Michigan, but now live in Chicago. Her work has appeared in *Columbia Poetry Review*, *Cream City Review*, the *Nashville Review*, the *New Orleans Review*, and *Whiskey Island*, among others. She is also the author of the books *Poems in Which You Die* (BatCat Press) and *Buick City* (Mayapple Press).

GEORGE DAVID CLARK is the author of *Reveille* (Arkansas, 2015), winner of the Miller Williams Prize. He edits the journal *32 Poems* and teaches creative writing at Washington and Jefferson College.

PATRICIA CLARK is Poet-in-Residence and Professor in the Department of Writing at Grand Valley State University. Author of five volumes of poetry, Patricia's latest book is *The Canopy*. Her work has been featured on *Poetry Daily* and *Verse Daily*, also appearing in *The Atlantic*, *Gettysburg Review*, *Poetry*, *Slate*, and *Stand*. Recent work appears in *Michigan Quarterly Review*, *Prairie Schooner*, *Superstition Review*, *Coal Hill Review*, *Salamander*, *The Boiler* (online) and the *Plume Anthology 4*. A chapbook of poems, *Wreath for the Red Admiral*, is newly out this summer from Spruce Alley Press.

Poet and essayist **HEIDI CZERWIEC** is the author of two recent chapbooks—*Sweet/Crude: A Bakken Boom Cycle* and *A Is For A-ke, The Chinese Monster*—and of the forthcoming poetry collection *Maternal*

Imagination, and the editor of *North Dakota Is Everywhere: An Anthology of Contemporary North Dakota Poets*.

DARREN C. DEMAREE is is the author of seven poetry collections, most recently *Unfinished Murder Ballads* (Jellyfish Highway, 2017). He is the Managing Editor of the *Best of the Net Anthology* and *Ovenbird Poetry*. He currently lives in Columbus, Ohio, with his wife and children.

LISA DORDAL is author of *Commemoration* (Finishing Line Press). A Pushcart Prize nominee and the recipient of an Academy of American Poets Prize, her poetry has appeared in a variety of journals, including *Best New Poets*, *Cave Wall*, *CALYX*, *Greensboro Review*, *Nimrod*, *Sojourners*, *New Millennium Writings*, and *The Journal of Feminist Studies in Religion*. She teaches in the English Department at Vanderbilt University.

SUSAN ELBE is the author of *The Map of What Happened*, winner of the 2012 Backwaters Press Prize and the 2014 Julie Suk Award from Jacar Press; *Eden in the Rearview Mirror* (Word Poetry); *Where Good Swimmers Drown*, winner of the 2011 Concrete Wolf Press Chapbook Contest; and *Light Made from Nothing* (Parallel Press).

LARA GEORGIEFF was born in St. Paul, Minnesota, and received an MFA in poetry from the Iowa Writers' Workshop. She lives in New York City.

JEREMY GLAZIER is a poet, an essayist, and Associate Professor of English at Ohio Dominican University, where he teaches poetry, the art of the essay, and popular courses on Emily Dickinson and Edgar Allan Poe. Over the past ten years, his poems have appeared in *Kenyon Review*, *Antioch Review*, *The Beloit Poetry Journal*, and many other literary journals. He has served as both a judge and a coach for Ohio's state-wide Poetry Out Loud competition, and he writes about poets and poetry for

The Los Angeles Review of Books. He is a two-time recipient of the Ohio Arts Council's Individual Excellence Award for Criticism.

MATTHEW GUENETTE is the author of two full-length poetry collections: *American Busboy* (University of Akron Press, 2011) and *Sudden Anthem* (Dream Horse Press, 2008). A third collection, *Vasectomania!*, is forthcoming in 2017 from the University of Akron Press as well as a chapbook, *Civil Disobedience* (winner of the Baltic Residency Chapbook Contest) from Rabbit Catastrophe Press. Matt lives, works, and loses sleep in Madison, WI.

MATT HART's most recent books are *Radiant Action* (H_NGM_N Books, 2016) and *Radiant Companion* (Monster House Press, 2016). A co-founder and the editor-in-chief of *Forklift, Ohio: A Journal of Poetry, Cooking & Light Industrial Safety*, he lives in Cincinnati where he is Associate Professor in Creative Writing and the Chair of Liberal Arts at the Art Academy of Cincinnati. He plays guitar and shouts in the bands TRAVEL and NEVERNEW.

REBECCA HAZELTON is the author of *Fair Copy* and *Vow*. Her poems have appeared in *Poetry, Southern Review, Boston Review, Best New Poets 2011*, and *Best American Poetry 2013* and *2015*, and the Pushcart anthology.

CYNTHIA MARIE HOFFMAN is the author of *Paper Doll Fetus* and *Sightseer*, as well as the chapbook *Her Human Costume*. Hoffman is a former Diane Middlebrook Poetry Fellow at the Wisconsin Institute for Creative Writing, Director's Guest at the Civitella Ranieri Foundation, and recipient of an Individual Artist Fellowship from the Wisconsin Arts Board. Her poems have appeared in *Jubilat, Pleiades, Fence, Blackbird, diode, The Journal*, and elsewhere.

KATHERINE L. HOLMES' poetry, short stories, and one-act plays have appeared in more than fifty journals, most recently in *Press Americana, Cider Press Review, Thin Air Magazine, Mused Literary Review, Red Booth Review, Wilderness House Literary Review, Blood Lotus, The Adirondack Review, Existere,* and *The Straddler.* In 2012, her short story collection, *Curiosity Killed the Sphinx and Other Stories,* was released by Hollywood Books International. More information is at her web site: https://sites. google.com/site/katherinelholmesauthorprofile.

LESLEY JENIKE is the author of full-length poetry collections *Ghost of Fashion* (CW Books) and *Holy Island* (to be rereleased by Gold Wake later this year), as well as chapbooks *How We Came Ashore* (Dancing Girl Press) and *Punctum* (forthcoming from Kent State University Press in 2017). Her poems have appeared in *Poetry, Southern Review, Gettysburg Review, Rattle, Smartish Pace, Waxwing, Blackbird, Passages North,* and many other journals. She's the recipient of awards, fellowships, and scholarships from the Ohio Arts Council, Kent State University Press, the Virginia Center for Creative Arts, the Vermont Studio Center, the Sewanee Writers' Conference, and the Academy of American Poets. She was awarded an M.F.A. from The Ohio State University in 2003 and a Ph.D. from the University of Cincinnati in 2008. She's currently Associate Professor of English at the Columbus College of Art and Design in Columbus, Ohio.

W. TODD KANEKO is the author of *The Dead Wrestler Elegies* (2014). His poems and prose have appeared in *Bellingham Review, Los Angeles Review, Barrelhouse, PANK, The Collagist,* and many other places. A recipient of fellowships from Kundiman and the *Kenyon Review* Writer's Workshop, he is currently coeditor of *Waxwing* and teaches at Grand Valley State University in Michigan.

SEAN KARNS has an MFA in creative writing from the University of Illinois and is the author of *Jar of Pennies*, a collection of poetry. His poetry has appeared or is forthcoming in the *Birmingham Poetry Review*, *Hobart*, *Rattle*, *Pleiades*, *Los Angeles Review*, *Cold Mountain Review*, *Folio*, and elsewhere

KATHLEEN KIRK is the author of six poetry chapbooks, most recently *ABCs of Women's Work* (Red Bird, 2015) and *Interior Sculpture* (dancing girl press, 2014). Her work appears in a number of print and online literary journals, including *Arsenic Lobster*, *The Fourth River*, *Fifth Wednesday*, *Flyway*, and *Poetry East*. She is the poetry editor for *Escape into Life*.

TED KOOSER was the United States Poet Laureate from 2004 to 2006 and won a Pulitzer Prize for his book of poems *Delights and Shadows*. He is the author of twelve full-length volumes of poetry and several books of nonfiction, and his work has appeared in many periodicals. He lives in Garland, Nebraska.

LEONARD KRESS has published fiction and poetry in *Massachusetts Review*, *Iowa Review*, *Crab Orchard Review*, *American Poetry Review*, *Harvard Review*, etc. His recent collections are *The Orpheus Complex*, *Living in the Candy Store*, and *Braids & Other Sestinas*. He teaches philosophy, religion, and creative writing at Owens College in Ohio and edits creative non-fiction for *Artful Dodge*.

Winner of *North American Review*'s 2015 Hearst Prize and past President of the Wisconsin Fellowship of Poets, MICHAEL KRIESEL judged the Science Fiction Poetry Association's 2016 contest. His poems have appeared in *Alaska Quarterly*, *Antioch Review*, *Rattle*, *Rosebud*, *The Progressive*, and *Wisconsin People & Ideas*. Read more of his work at http://www.righthandpointing.net/michael-kriesel-every-name

C. Kubasta experiments with hybrid forms, excerpted text, and shifting voices—her work has been called claustrophobic and unflinching. Her favorite rejection (so far) noted that one editor loved her work, and the other hated it. A six-year-old once mistook her for Velma, from *Scooby Doo*, and was unduly excited. She feels a strong affinity for Skipper, Barbie's flat-footed cousin. For each major publication, she celebrates with a new tattoo; someday she hopes to be completely sleeved—her skin a labyrinth of signifiers, utterly opaque. Find her at ckubasta.com.

Michael Levan has work in recent or forthcoming issues of *45th Parallel Magazine*, *Iron Horse Literary Review*, *Copper Nickel*, *Ruminate*, and *Hunger Mountain*. He is an Assistant Professor of English at the University of Saint Francis and writes reviews for *American Microreviews and Interviews*. He lives in Fort Wayne, Indiana, with his wife, Molly, and children, Atticus and Dahlia.

Sandra Lindow has published seven collections of her poetry. Her awards include two WWA first prize Jade Ring Awards, the WFOP Triad Theme Award, the 1990 CWW Posner Award for best poetry collection by a Wisconsin writer, and the Wisconsin Press Women's Award for Poetry. Lindow is west central regional VP of the Wisconsin Fellowship of Poets. She is semi-retired and lives, teaches, writes and edits in Menomonie, Wisconsin.

D. A. Lockhart is the author of *This City at the Crossroads* (Black Moss Press, 2017) and *Big Medicine Comes to Erie* (Black Moss Press, 2016). His work has appeared in numerous journals including the *Malahat Review*, *Hawai'i Review*, OSU's *The Journal*, the *Windsor Review*, and *Contemporary Verse 2*. Lockhart is a graduate of the Indiana University-Bloomington MFA in Creative Writing program and a one-time resident of Indiana that carries his Hoosier connection with considerable pride.

He is a member of the Moravian of the Thames First Nation that lives on Odawa land that is now occupied by the Pillette Village neighbourhood.

KAREN LOEB's poetry and fiction have appeared in *Hanging Loose*, *Thema*, *The Main Street Rag*, *Bloodroot*, *New Ohio Review*, and other magazines. Poems are forthcoming in *The Cape Rock*, *Otis Nebula*, and *Allegro Poetry*. One of her stories won a 2014 Editor's Choice award in the Raymond Carver Short Story Contest. Another story won first place in the 2014 Wisconsin People and Ideas Fiction Contest.

AMIT MAJMUDAR is a novelist, poet, essayist, and diagnostic nuclear radiologist (M.D.). He writes and practices in Dublin, Ohio, where he lives with his wife, twin sons, and baby daughter.

MICHAEL MARBERRY poetry has appeared in *The New Republic*, *West Branch*, *Sycamore Review*, *Bat City Review*, *Hayden's Ferry Review*, *Guernica*, *Verse Daily*, and elsewhere. He has received a Pushcart Prize and has been a finalist for The National Poetry Series. He received his MFA from Ohio State University and is currently pursuing his PhD at Western Michigan University, where he coordinates the Poets-in-Print Reading Series.

MATT MAUCH is the author of *Bird~Brain*, *If You're Lucky Is a Theory of Mine*, *Prayer Book*, and the chapbook *The Brilliance of the Sparrow*. His poems have appeared in numerous journals, including *Conduit*, *H_NGM_N*, *DIAGRAM*, *Willow Springs*, the *Los Angeles Review*, *Forklift*, *Ohio*, *Sonora Review*, *Water~Stone Review*, and on the *Poetry Daily* and *Verse Daily* websites. Mauch leads the staff at *Poetry City, USA*, a journal of poetry and prose on poetry, and lives in Minneapolis, where he teaches in the AFA in Creative Writing program at Normandale Community College.

JOHN MCCARTHY is the author of *Ghost County* (Midwestern Gothic Press, 2016). His work appears in *Best New Poets 2015*, *Redivider*, *the minnesota review*, *RHINO*, *The Pinch*, and *Salamander*. In the summer of 2016, John was a writer-in-residence at the Gullkistan Center for Creativity in Iceland.

Poet and writer **KEVIN MCKELVEY** grew up near Lebanon, Indiana, and graduated from DePauw University and Southern Illinois University Carbondale. Some of his Charles C. Deam Wilderness Area poems have been published in *Dream Wilderness*, a chapbook, and a full-length book of the same name is forthcoming in 2017. His poems, essays, stories, and blogs have appeared in numerous journals, anthologies, and online venues. He recently completed a bookmap of the Upper White River Watershed in Indiana, and he is also at work on a novel. Other work focuses on social practice art, digital media, or environmental sustainability, and he teaches in those areas and in the English Department at the University of Indianapolis where he is an Associate Professor. He lives with his wife and three children in Indianapolis in a house built in the 1870s and can be found online at kevinmckelvey.org.

MICHELLE MENTING is the author of *Leaves Surface Like Skin* (Terrapin Books, 2017) and two poetry chapbooks. Her work has been published in the *Cimarron Review*, *The Offing*, *Southeast Review*, *American Life in Poetry*, and *Midwestern Gothic*, among other places. Originally from northern Wisconsin and Upper Michigan, she earned an MFA from Northern Michigan University and a PhD from the University of Nebraska. She currently lives in mid-coast Maine and can be found online at www.michellementing.com.

MARY MERIAM's first full-length collection, *Conjuring My Leafy Muse*, was nominated for the Poets' Prize. Her poems have appeared in twelve anthologies, including *Measure for Measure: An Anthology of Poetic Meters*

(Penguin Random House, 2015), and many publications, including *Literary Imagination, American Life in Poetry, Cimarron Review, Rattle,* and *The New York Times.*

PAMELA MILLER has been writing, publishing and performing her poetry in Chicago for almost 40 years. She is the author of four books of poems, most recently *Miss Unthinkable* (Mayapple Press, 2013). Her work has appeared in *RHINO, Blue Fifth Review, Olentangy Review, Circe's Lament: Anthology of Wild Women Poetry, Caravel, After Hours,* and many other journals and anthologies.

TRACY MISHKIN is a call center veteran with a PhD and an MFA student in Creative Writing at Butler University. She is the author of two chapbooks, I Almost Didn't Make It to McDonald's (Finishing Line Press, 2014) and The Night I Quit Flossing (Five Oaks Press, 2016). She has been nominated for a Pushcart Prize.

JULIA ANNA MORRISON is a poet from Alpharetta, Georgia. She has an MFA from the Iowa Writers' Workshop. In 2014, Julia was a Nightboat Books Poetry Prize finalist and a Yaddo Residency Fellow. You can find more of her work in Handsome, LARB Quarterly Journal or at www.juliaannamorrison.com.

CJ MUCHHALA is the author of the chapbook *Traveling Without a Map.* Her poems have appeared in numerous print and online journals, anthologies, art exhibits, on CD-ROM and audio CD. She has been nominated for the *Best of the Net* and Pushcart awards. She lives in Shorewood, Wisconsin.

RICHARD NEWMAN is the author of the poetry collections *All the Wasted Beauty of the World* (Able Muse Press, 2014), *Domestic Fugues* (Steel Toe Books, 2009), and *Borrowed Towns* (Word Press, 2005). His novel

Graveyard of the Gods will appear this fall (Bank Slate Press, 2016). For twenty-two years he edited *River Styx* and directed the *River Styx* Reading Series. He currently teaches at the College of Marshall Islands.

ELIZABETH O'BRIEN lives in Minneapolis, MN, where she earned an MFA in Poetry at the University of Minnesota. Her work—poetry and prose—has appeared in many literary journals, including *New England Review, DIAGRAM, Sixth Finch, Whiskey Island, decomP, PANK, CutBank, Ampersand Review, Revolver, Swink,* and *Versal.*

EVA OLSGARD (BA Bard College) is a Norwegian-American writer, artist, and designer. In addition to performing and exhibiting her work internationally, she pioneers award-winning programming and lectures on the arts and cultural studies. Her writing has appeared in: *Pinyon Review, Cobalt Review,* and *Magma Poetry* (UK). Her Buddhist instillation, *Prayers for a City of Pollen and Light,* was commissioned for Chicago's Gross Park Sculpture Invitational. Her cubist poem, "EYE DISCRIMINATE AGAINST GAZE" (2005-ongoing), launched on Myspace.com/focalength as an interactive "bust" and on T-shirts donned by acclaimed poets and authors provoking a world wide discussion about xenophobia, surveillance, and social media.

DEONTE OSAYANDE is a former track and field sprinter turned writer from Detroit, Michigan. He writes essays and his poems have been nominated for the *Best of the Net Anthology,* a Pushcart Prize, and published in numerous publications. He has represented Detroit at multiple National Poetry Slam competitions. He's currently a professor of English at Wayne County Community College and teaches youth through the Inside Out Detroit Literary Arts Program.

DONNA PUCCIANI has published poetry on four continents and is the author of seven books of poetry. Her work has been translated into

Chinese, Japanese, Italian and German, and has won awards from the Illinois Arts Council, Poets and Patrons of Chicago, The National Federation of State Poetry Societies, and Poetry on the Lake, among others. She served as Vice President of the Poets' Club of Chicago for over a decade.

DIVYA RAJAN'S works as a regulatory scientist and was poetry editor at *The Furnace Review*. Her works have appeared in the *Silk and Spice* anthology, *After Hours, Gloom Cupboard, Missouri Review, Berfrois*, and *The Missed Slate*, among other publications. Her work has also received nominations for the Pushcart and Best of the Net.

JULIAN RANDALL is a Living Queer Black poet from Chicago. He is a 2016 *Callaloo* fellow, Lois Morrell Poetry Prize winner and the 2015 National College Slam (CUPSI) Best Poet. He is also a cofounder of the Afrolatinx poetry collective Piel Cafe. His work has appeared or is forthcoming in *The Offing, Winter Tangerine Review, Vinyl, Puerto del Sol*, and *African Voices*. He is a candidate for his MFA in Poetry at Ole Miss.

RITA MAE REESE is the author of *The Alphabet Conspiracy* (Arktoi Books) and *The Book of Hulga*, which was selected by Denise Duhamel for the Felix Pollak Prize. She is a recipient of a Rona Jaffe Foundation Writers' Award, a Stegner fellowship in fiction, a "Discovery"/*The Nation* award, and a Pamaunok Poetry Prize, among other awards. She is a co-director of literary arts at the Arts & Literature Laboratory in Madison, Wisconsin. She can be found at www.ritamaereese.com.

ANDREW RUZKOWSI'S poems have appeared or are forthcoming in *Columbia Poetry Review, The Bakery, [PANK], Midwestern Gothic, The Seattle Review, Willows Wept Review, The Camel Saloon, Emerge Literary Journal*, and *Parable Press*, among others. He has been nominated for two Pushcart Prizes, a *Best of the Net* award, and was a finalist for the 2012

Atlantis Award and the 2012 Kay Murphy Prize for Poetry. His debut chapbook, *A Shape & Sound*, is available from ELJ Publications. His first full-length collection, *Things That Keep Us from Drifting*, is available from Another New Calligraphy. He also serves as the reviews editor for *Poets' Quarterly*, and as a poetry editor for *Black Tongue Review*.

MAX SCHLEICHER's poetry has appeared in *Prelude*, *Squawk Back*, and *Zocalo Public Square*. He grew up in Milwaukee and now lives in Chicago.

MAGGIE SMITH is the author of three books of poetry: *Good Bones* (Tupelo Press, 2017); *The Well Speaks of Its Own Poison* (Tupelo Press, 2015); and *Lamp of the Body* (Red Hen Press, 2005). Smith is also the author of three prizewinning chapbooks. Her poems appear in *Best American Poetry*, *the New York Times*, *The Paris Review*, *Ploughshares*, *The Gettysburg Review*, *Guernica*, *Plume*, *AGNI*, *Virginia Quarterly Review*, and elsewhere. In 2016, her poem "Good Bones" went viral internationally and has been translated into nearly a dozen languages. PRI (Public Radio International) called it "the official poem of 2016." Smith has received fellowships from the National Endowment for the Arts, the Ohio Arts Council, and the Sustainable Arts Foundation, among others. She lives in Bexley, Ohio, and is a freelance writer and editor.

EMILY STODDARD is a writer of poetry and prose, born and raised in Michigan. Her poems have appeared in *Menacing Hedge*, *Cactus Heart*, and *Big Scream*, and she also has a short story forthcoming in the anthology *An Alphabet of Embers*. After residing in San Francisco for two years, Emily has replanted in her home state, where she's falling in love again with the four seasons.

BRUCE TAYLOR is the author of eight collections of poetry, including *The Longest You've Lived Anywhere: New & Selected Poems*, and editor of eight anthologies including *Wisconsin Poetry* (Wisconsin Academy of Science, Arts & Letters). His poetry has appeared in such places as *Able Muse, The Chicago Review, The Cortland Review, The Nation, The New York Quarterly, Poetry, Rattle, Rosebud,* and on the *Writer's Almanac.* He lives in Lake Hallie, Wisconsin, with his wife, the writer Patti See.

JESSICA THOMPSON's poetry has appeared in journals such as *The Sow's Ear* and *Atlanta Review,* as well as in *Circe's Lament: Anthology of Wild Women Poetry* (Accents Publishing). She is also the author of the chapbook *Bullets and Blank Bibles* (Liquid Paper Press).

JAMES TOLAN is author of *Mass of the Forgotten* (Autumn House Press), *Red Walls* (Dos Madres Press), and co-editor with Holly Messitt of *New America: Contemporary Literature for a Changing Society* (Autumn House Press). His poems appear in such journals as *American Literary Review, Atlanta Review, Indiana Review, Ploughshares,* and *Verse Daily.* Originally from Chicago, he lives in Brooklyn and is Professor of English at the City University of New York/BMCC. To learn more, please visit his website: www.jamestolan.com.

STEVE TOMASKO doesn't fish as much, walk in the woods enough, or write as often as he should. His first chapbook, *and no spiders were harmed,* was published by Red Bird Chapbooks in 2015. Steve and his wife, Jeanie, were editors of the *2015 Wisconsin Poets' Calendar.* Although they live in Middleton, Wisconsin, their hearts reside near Lake Superior.

COREY VAN LANDINGHAM is the author of *Antidote,* winner of the 2012 Ohio State University Press/*The Journal* Award in Poetry. A recipient of a 2017 National Endowment for the Arts Fellowship and a Wallace Stegner Fellowship from Stanford University, her work has appeared in *Best American Poetry 2014, Boston Review, Kenyon Review,* and *The New*

Yorker, among many other places. She's currently a doctoral student in English Literature and Creative Writing at the University of Cincinnati, and a Book Review Editor for *Kenyon Review*.

LISA VIHOS' poems have appeared in *Big Muddy, Forge, The Main Street Rag, Mom Egg Review, Seems, Verse Wisconsin*, and many other journals. She has two Pushcart Prize nominations and two chapbooks, *A Brief History of Mail* (Pebblebrook Press, 2011) and *The Accidental Present* (Finishing Line Press, 2012). She is the poetry and arts editor for *Stoneboat Literary Journal*, an occasional guest blogger for *The Best American Poetry*, and the Sheboygan organizer for 100 Thousand Poets for Change. She loves cooking, bicycling, listening to her teenage son play guitar, and walking along Lake Michigan, not necessarily in that order.

CLAIRE WAHMANHOLM's poems have most recently appeared in, or are forthcoming from, *Paperbag, Saltfront, PANK, Bennington Review, Birdfeast, Memorious, The Collapsar, Bateau*, and *The Kenyon Review Online*. Her chapbook, *Night Vision*, won the 2017 New Michigan Press/ *DIAGRAM* chapbook contest and is forthcoming in November 2017. Her debut full-length collection is forthcoming from Tinderbox Editions in early 2019. She lives and teaches in the Twin Cities.

JOHN WALSER has lived most of his life in the upper Midwest. An associate professor at Marian University, he holds a doctorate in English and Creative Writing from the University of Wisconsin-Milwaukee. A Pushcart nominee as well as a recipient of the Lorine Niedecker Poetry Award, John was a semi-finalist for the 2013 and the 2016 Pablo Neruda Prize. His poetry has appeared in numerous journals, including *Nimrod, Spillway, Superstition Review*, and *december magazine*. He lives in Fond du Lac, Wisconsin, with his girlfriend, Julie, who is his first reader and his best reader.

TIMOTHY WALSH's most recent poetry collections are *When the World Was Rear-Wheel Drive* and *The Book of Arabella*. His awards include the Grand Prize in the *Atlanta Review* International Poetry Competition, the Kurt Vonnegut Fiction Prize from *North American Review*, the New Jersey Poets Prize, and the Wisconsin Academy Fiction Prize. He is the author of a book of literary criticism, *The Dark Matter of Words: Absence, Unknowing, and Emptiness in Literature* (Southern Illinois University Press) and two poetry chapbooks, *Wild Apples* (Parallel Press) and *Blue Lace Colander* (Marsh River Editions). Find more at: http://timothyawalsh.com/

TORI GRANT WELHOUSE writes poems and lists. She is an active volunteer for the Wisconsin Fellowship of Poets (www.wfop.org) and coordinates the poetry reading series HOTT (www.houseofthetomato.com). She earned an MFA from Antioch International in London. Raised within cheering distance of Lambeau Field in Green Bay, Wisconsin, Tori now lives in farm fields, next to a meandering river, with a husband who thinks he's a lumberjack. More at www.torigrantwelhouse.com.

MARK WILLIAMS' poems have appeared in *The Southern Review*, *The Hudson Review*, *Nimrod*, *Rattle*, and *New Poetry from the Midwest 2014*. In 2015, his chapbook *Happiness* was published by Finishing Line Press. His fiction has appeared in *Indiana Review* and his story, "One Something Happy Family," was a finalist in a recent competition at *Glimmer Train*. Williams has lived in Indiana for the past 40 years.

HANIF WILLIS-ABDURRAQIB is a poet, essayist, and cultural critic from Columbus, Ohio. He is a poetry editor at *Muzzle Magazine*, a columnist at *MTV News*, and a *Callaloo* creative writing fellow. His first collection of poems, *The Crown Ain't Worth Much*, was released by Button Poetry/Exploding Pinecone Press in 2016.

TESS WILSON's poems have previously been published in *NEAT Magazine*, *Inscape Magazine*, and the annual Free Poems series. She earned her MFA in Creative Writing from Chatham University and currently serves as assistant editor of Hyacinth Girl Press and reader/carpenter for the Pittsburgh Poetry Houses project. Previously, she was an associate editor and online layout designer of *The Fourth River*, editor/designer of *This Time: An Anthology*, and a poetry editor of *Inscape Magazine*.

SARAH ANN WINN was born and raised in Akron, Ohio. Her first book, *Alma Almanac*, won the 2016 Barrow Street Book Prize, selected by Elaine Equi. It will be published by Barrow Street Press in 2017. She is the author of five chapbooks, the most recent of which is *Ever After the End Matter* (Hermeneutic Chaos, 2017). Her poems, prose, and hybrid works have appeared in *Five Points*, *Hayden's Ferry Review*, *Massachusetts Review*, *Passages North*, and *Quarterly West*, among others. She holds a Master of Fine Arts from George Mason University and a Master of Library Science from Catholic University of America. Visit her at http://bluebirdwords.com or follow her @blueaisling.

DAVID WINTER is the recipient of a 2016 Individual Excellence Award from the Ohio Arts Council and a 2016-18 Stadler Fellowship from Bucknell University. He wrote the poetry chapbook *Safe House* (Thrush Press, 2013), and his poems also appear in magazines such as *The Baffler*; *Forklift, Ohio*; *Meridian*; *Ninth Letter*; and *The Offing*.

SCOTT WOODS is the author of *Urban Contemporary History Month* and *We Over Here Now* (Brick Cave Books, 2016 and 2013 respectively) and has published and edited work in a variety of publications. He has been featured multiple times in national press, including multiple appearances on National Public Radio. He was the President of Poetry Slam Inc. and emcees the Writers' Block Poetry Night, an open mic series in Columbus,

Ohio. In April 2006, he became the first poet to ever complete a 24-hour solo poetry reading, a feat he bested with seven more annual readings without repeating a single poem.

SERIES
EDITORS

OKLA ELLIOTT (1977-2017) was an Illinois Distinguished Fellow at the University of Illinois, where he worked in the fields of comparative literature and trauma studies. He also held an MFA from Ohio State University. His nonfiction, poetry, short fiction, and translations have appeared in journals and magazines such as *Another Chicago Magazine, Harvard Review, Indiana Review, The Literary Review, New York Quarterly, Prairie Schooner, A Public Space,* and *Subtropics,* among others. His books include a story collection, *From the Crooked Timber* (Press 53, 2011), a poetry collection, *The Cartographer's Ink* (NYQ Press, 2014), and the novel *The Doors You Mark Are Your Own* (co-authored with Raul Clement, Curbside Splendor, 2015). His book of translation, *Blackbirds in September: Selected Shorter Poems of Jürgen Becker,* was released by Black Lawrence in 2015. A co-founder of New American Press, *MAYDAY Magazine,* and the blog of political and literary commentary *As It Ought to Be,* Okla was a passionate and tireless advocate for literature, publishing, social justice, and considered public opinion.

HANNAH STEPHENSON is a poet, editor, and instructor living in Columbus, Ohio (where she also runs a literary event series called *Paging Columbus*). She is the author of *Cadence* (which won the Ohio Chapbook Prize from the Wick Poetry Center) and *In the Kettle, the Shriek*; series Co-Editor of *New Poetry from the Midwest*; and her writing has appeared in *The Atlantic, The Huffington Post, 32 Poems, The Journal,* and *Poetry Daily.* You can visit her online at *The Storialist* (www.thestorialist.com).

2017 HEARTLAND POETRY PRIZE FINAL JUDGE

KATHY FAGAN's collections include *Lip* (Carnegie Mellon UP, 2009) and *Sycamore* (Milkweed Editions, 2017). She is the author of the National Poetry Series selection *The Raft* (Dutton, 1985), the Vassar Miller Prize winner *MOVING & ST RAGE* (Univ of North Texas, 1999), and *The Charm* (Zoo, 2002). Her work has appeared in *The Paris Review, The Kenyon Review, Slate, FIELD, Narrative, The New Republic*, and *Poetry*, among other literary magazines, and is widely anthologized. Fagan is the recipient of awards and fellowships from the Ingram Merrill Foundation, the National Endowment for the Arts, The Frost Place, Ohioana, and the Ohio Arts Council. The Director of Creative Writing and the MFA Program at The Ohio State University, she is currently Professor of English, Poetry Editor of OSU Press, and Advisor to *The Journal*.

CPSIA information can be obtained
at www.ICGtesting.com
Printed in the USA
FFOW03n2240220118
44648517-44606FF